"And In One Holy Local Church"?

The Ghettoization of Protestantism

A Critique of Modern Views of
Mandatory Local Church Membership

Bojidar Marinov

Dallas, Georgia

"One Holy Local Church"?
The Ghettoization of Protestantism

Published by **New Liberty Mission, LLC**

www.NewLibertyMission.com

Printed in the United States of America

ISBN: 978-1-63587-039-8

Contents

1. Introduction

I need to start with a disclaimer: while this article began a commentary on a quotation by Jeff Durbin, pastor of Apologia Church, Tempe, Arizona, it is *not* in any way an assessment of the person of Jeff Durbin, and it is *not* in any way an assessment of his ministry, nor is that the focus. I know very little about his person (having met him only once), and I know even less about his ministry. I don't follow it, and what I know, I know from testimonies of other people. I get the general impression that it is a good and legitimate ministry, beneficial to a number of people.

I also should say about the specific quotation I will be discussing, I don't know what its specific context is. It is a Facebook status, so one can only guess what the context is. My guess, given some developments of the last couple of years, is that the quotation was directed against Abolish Human Abortion (AHA), for some of the specific accusations closely match the accusations Jeff and his associates have been leveling against AHA. I am not trying to defend AHA here, although, I must mention, I have never been able to understand this bitter hostility against them; and neither do I understand the accusations against them. I know Jeff Durbin has his own pro-life organization which he is trying to get off the ground, and I heartily hope and pray he succeeds; but why it has to go with bashing AHA still evades me. It may become clear after reading this booklet.

As part of this disclaimer, I am indeed partial to AHA for many reasons. One is personal: all of my best friends are Abolitionists. Another is missional: They achieve results, and that at almost zero cost. Another one is ethical: These are courageous folks, and I value courage anywhere I see it. Another one I could call "psychological": I prefer to work in a setting of equal-in-rank co-workers, each of whom knows what he is doing; I get tired in an environment of "leaders" and "followers." I reject the "leader-follower" model even in my mission field in Bulgaria, where everyone believes I am a "leader" because I have founded the mission. AHA is exactly that kind of organization of co-workers, which exactly suits my preferences. So I admit, I am partial. But then again, I may be mistaken, and the quotation may not be even related to them. Either way, none of the following analysis is personal, and none is addressed at Jeff Durbin's ministry. So, if any reader is quick to take offense, relax, sit down, and read what I *really* have to say.

What is more important is that the quotation has certain theological and ecclesiological content. And this content is based on certain presuppositions, as well as certain historical origins. It also leads to certain practical conclusions. What I argue in this article is that the quotation displays a particular theology, peculiar to *Baptists,* that many have adopted *by inertia,* and which has become the dominant paradigm in the modern Reformed churches, but also that few have stopped to consider either its presuppositions or the conclusions from enatiled by it. The London Confession (as we shall see) carries an ecclesiology that has been introduced only recently in the Reformed world, is based on a fallacious ideology, and has proven destructive to the Reformed churches. So, my purpose with this article is to invite Jeff Durbin to consider the origin and the destructive consequences of that ecclesiology and change his commitments and beliefs accordingly. I need to add, I would not have paid attention to what he said if it wasn't brought to my desk by at least a dozen friends who asked me for my opinion. So I guess the quotation has gained some popularity—and therefore the dangers of its fallacious theology need to be addressed to prevent future destruction to the church.

Jeff's direct words are as follows:

> Facebook is filled with "Facebook Prophets". These are people who aren't a part of the local church but insist on giving biblical insight and wisdom to those who are actually a part of God's design for believers: corporate worship, communion, under the care of pastors, etc. The Bible can be a dangerous thing in the hands of those who despise authority, aren't involved in the life of the body, and act like renegades. We are wise to avoid the "insight" of people who refuse to participate in the most fundamental part of the life of a Christian: the local church. God gave us one another for a reason. If we don't love the church, we don't love Jesus.

The sentiment is nothing new (although, it is relatively new in church history, as we will see), and it is accepted *by inertia* by almost every single person today who in one way or another attains to some position of authority in the church—or, rather, to be more precise, some position of *legal power* in the church.[1] This sentiment is based on several assumptions. *First,* it assumes that the local church is the same thing as the church—hence the keen emphasis the local church. *Second,* it assumes that the visible and the invisible church are identical. *Third,* it assumes that being under formally ordained church government is mandatory—and if one is not, therefore he "despises authority." And *fourth,* it assumes that God will only correct His Church through formally instituted human bureaucracies within the church, and never through other means.

1. As I argue in my article, "Modern Presbyterianism and the Destruction of the Principle of Plurality of Elders," there is a difference between authority and legal power, and modern churches have replaced authority with power. http://www.christendomrestored.com/blog/2016/02/modern-presbyterianism-and-the-destruction-of-the-principle-of-plurality-of-elders/

All these, in the final account, rest on one single concept: the doctrine of "local church membership." Or, as it is known in some Reformed churches today, "local church covenant." Remove that concept, and the above four assumptions disintegrate. So, I will focus my analysis on the concept of *mandatory* "local church membership"—its history, its theology, and its consequences—and will also cover the above assumptions.

2. Baptist Half-Way Confessionalism

In the insistence on local church membership, or "being part of the local church," it looks like Jeff Durbin is in accord with the Baptist tradition and Reformed Baptist confessionalism. Mandatory "local church membership" is indeed an integral part of the Baptist tradition. And it's not just tradition. It is in fact specifically codified in what we can call The Last Great Reformed Baptist Confession, namely, the London Baptist Confession of Faith of 1689.

The 1689 Baptist Confession was based on the Westminster Confession of 1647, and follows it almost word for word, except in the chapter for baptism, and in a few other places, specifically the chapter, "Of the Church" (ch. 25 in the WCF; ch. 26 in the LBCF). The changes in that chapter are enormously significant. Where the WCF speaks in only six articles and sees nothing more than the universal church, leaving the issue of local congregations to non-confessional standards, the LBCF has 15 articles, of which 11 specifically outline the form, the membership, the government, and many other specific features of local churches. This is a very clear line of separation between Presbyterian/Congregationalist confessionalism on one hand and Baptist confessionalism on the other. Contrary to what many assume, Presbyterianism allows for much greater liberty when it comes to ecclesiastical forms—even though we will see later that modern Presbyterian denominations differ substantially in their view of church government and membership. As for Baptists, they are confessionally bound to a very specific view of church membership by their own Confession. The language is particularly strong in this regard:

> In the execution of this power wherewith he is so intrusted, the Lord Jesus calleth out of the world unto himself, through the ministry of his word, by his Spirit, those that are given unto him by his Father, that they may walk before him in all the ways of obedience, which he prescribeth to them in his word. Those thus called, *he commandeth to walk together in particular societies, or churches,* for their mutual edification, and the due performance of that public worship, which he requireth of them in the world (LBCF 26:5; emphasis added).

The Confession does not offer a single Bible verse which plainly teaches such a "command." Later Baptist theologians admit that there is no such Biblical verse. Even John Macarthur, for all his insistence on "church membership," admits that the Bible never speaks of it.[2] Modern Presbyterian theologians who support the concept of mandatory "local church membership" also admit that there is no verse that explicitly teaches such "local church membership." The strongest Biblical argument for such "membership" that was used at the time was Acts 2:41–42; but the text clearly does *not* speak of such local church covenant. (How exactly did they organize a "local church" of thousands of people, out of all those diverse nations, within the narrow constraints of Jerusalem?) Nowhere else in the Bible is there anything to suggest any form of special covenantal commitment to a local body that is different, separate from, or superadded to the Covenant of Grace made with the universal church in general in baptism.

Keep in mind, this was written by the same group which

---

2. "Scripture does not contain an explicit command to formally join a local church. . . ." http://www.gty.org/resources/distinctives/DD03/church-membership.

rejected infant baptism because they did not see any specific command for it in Scripture. It sounds schizophrenic that they would mandate local church membership without an explicit command in Scripture. We will see later why the English Baptists had to go down this road. For now, *let's remember that Confessions, while important, are not perfectly reliable.* They are always a mixture of correct and incorrect interpretations, they often have current pragmatic considerations included in them, and they are often self-contradictory, especially in those parts where they deviate from the Word of God, or try to force an interpretation on it.

Even if we ignore for now this lack of Biblical proofs, another problem appears. While Baptist churches today may insist on the membership clause of the Confession, they avoid abiding by another clause: that of leadership. The question is: *how does one define such a local congregation*? One can become a member of any congregation, but more importantly, how does one know which congregation is a real congregation? How do we know that Apologia is a real congregation? Obviously, being a "member" of just anything that claims to be a "local congregation" will not do: can one be a member of a Mormon "congregation"? The LBCF has a definition, and it is a definition based specifically on *distinction of classes* within the local congregation:

> A particular church, gathered and completely organized according to the mind of Christ, consists of officers and members; and the officers appointed by Christ to be chosen and set apart by the church (so called and gathered), for the peculiar administration of ordinances, and execution of power or duty, which he intrusts them with, or calls them to, to be continued to the end of the world, are bishops or elders, and deacons (LBCF 26:8).

The existence of elders in the church, therefore, makes it

legitimate. But how are they chosen? How do we know that certain particular elders are legitimate and therefore their particular church is legitimate? How do we know that Jeff Durbin is a legitimate elder whose ministry makes his local church legitimate? The very next article gives the Baptist answer:

> The way appointed by Christ for the calling of any person, fitted and gifted by the Holy Spirit, unto the office of bishop or elder in a church, is, that *he be chosen thereunto by the common suffrage of the church itself*; and solemnly set apart by fasting and prayer, *with imposition of hands of the eldership of the church, if there be any before constituted therein*. . . . [emphasis added.]

So, here is the argument: You must join a local church. You will know it is a local church if it has elders. If it doesn't have elders, it can appoint itself elders, and thus will be a local church.

Problem: before it has elders, is it a church? If it is, why does the Confession say otherwise? If it is not—because it doesn't have elders—what are you joining, and why? The authors of the LCBF, obviously, deviated from the Bible by placing on their flocks and members a burden that the Bible does not. But any such deviation from the Bible inevitably creates logical contradictions in thought and practice. Thus, they created a conundrum for future generations of Baptists. The result is that no one really knows whether a group that calls itself a "Baptist church" is really a Baptist *church*. Is Apologia a real church? If yes, by what standard? Because it has elders? Are these elders legitimate? How do we know? How does Jeff know that the people he criticizes are "not part of a local church"? By the standard of the LBCF, in any group of at least two, if one of them is "chosen thereunto by the common suffrage of the church itself," such a person is just as much a legitimate elder as Jeff Durbin. Or, otherwise, just as much an *illegitimate* elder as Jeff Durbin, depending on which direction we be consistent.

This conundrum is well-known to all Baptist ministers who claim to be confessional. No one can know if any of them are really legitimate church ministers. Is John McArthur legitimate? Who knows? Is Franklin Graham legitimate? Was he "chosen thereunto" by his father . . . but is his father legitimate? That is why, when it comes to chapter 26, all "confessional" Baptist ministers are actually *half*-confessional: confessional when they impose the burden of "membership" on their members, but silent when they must prove their own authority is legitimate in any consistent way. In the final account, it is often one's media presence and influence that "legitimizes" a minister. This conundrum, therefore, is also where the origin of the modern celebrity worship is.

The early Baptists understood this conundrum and sought a solution. Originally, the solution was to return to the Roman and Eastern Orthodox argument of "apostolic succession." Believe it or not, for two and half centuries, Baptists held to the same view of legitimacy of authority as the Papists: a succession of laying on of hands in Baptist churches from the time of Christ to our own day. (In fact, I remember a Baptist missionary in Bulgaria in the early 1990s, arguing with an Eastern Orthodox priest as to who had a greater claim to apostolic succession.) The theory was called "Baptist perpetuity" and was extremely popular among the rank-and-file Baptists in the United States. In the second half of the 19th century, a number of Baptist scholars started refuting this as a myth. The change was not always peaceful. William Whitsitt, professor at the Southern Baptist Theological Seminary, was forced to resign in 1899, after he proved from historical sources that English Baptists did not practice immersion before 1641. Even after the theory of Baptist perpetuity was thoroughly refuted by scholars, the myth continued to live on at the popular level. In 1931,

James Milton Carroll, a Baptist pastor from Texas, published a small book which remains popular among many Baptists to this day: *The Trail of Blood*. In it, he made the case for an unbroken succession of Baptist churches and ministers from the Apostles. His list of Baptists in history, however, included even openly heretical groups like the Cathari, the Albigenses, the Paulicians, etc. As strange as it sounds that a Baptist minister might countenance such groups, in our day, John MacArthur has recognized such connections with heretical groups in the past.[3] There is a good reason for it: apostolic succession seems to solve the conundrum planted in the Confession. At the cost of consistency, however.

Historical evidence against this myth of Baptist perpetuity was too strong to be ignored, and in the 20th century, the majority of Baptists abandoned it. The Baptist Affirmation of Faith of 1966, a modern restatement of the LBCF by Reformed Baptists, completely omits the mention of "imposition of hands" by already existing eldership. This means it is all election by the congregation now:

> The appointment of elders (including pastors) and deacons, for office within the local church, and of preachers and missionaries for the work of evangelism is the responsibility of the local church under the guidance of the Holy Spirit. The Lord's ordination is recognised both by the experience of the inward conviction, and by the approval of the church observing the possession of those gifts and graces required by Scripture for the office concerned. The one so called should be set apart by the prayer of the whole church (Baptist Affirmation of Faith, 1966 "The Doctrine of the Church," Art. 5).

3. See James F. Stitzinger, "The History of Expository Preaching," in *Preaching: How to Preach Biblically*, ed. by John MacArthur (Nashville, TN: Thomas Nelson, Inc., 2005).

This does not solve the logical and theological problem, though. Of course, we first have the issue of just dropping a basic Biblical doctrine, "laying on of hands," mentioned among the "elementary teachings" in Hebrews 6:1–2. We also return to the originally stated contradiction: if a local church is validated by having elders, yet elders are simply elected by the local church, then there is no way to accuse anyone of being "separated from the body" (aside from a legitimate excommunication—more on that later). All one has to do is have one more professing Christan with them, and both elect an "elder" between them. If this is legitimate (confessionally, it would be), then ultimately *everyone who believes is by default a member of the body*, and therefore all accusations otherwise are false accusations and sin. If it is not legitimate, then the accuser first needs to prove the legitimacy of his own "local congregation" by the same satandard. Such proof is not logically possible under the confessional standards of modern Reformed Baptists. As we just saw, after centuries of trying to make their Confession work through *formal apostolic* legitimacy, they have even dropped that and therefore have returned to the circular standard just outlined. Either everyone is a legitimate believer, or no Baptist congregation is legitimate at all, and therefore no Baptist is a true believer. This happens when you try to impose non-Biblical burdens on God's elect.

For this reason, most "confessional" Baptists today prefer to not talk about this part of their Confession. As we saw in the Baptist Affirmation of Faith of 1966, they even feel free to modify it and omit the inconvenient parts of it. Baptist "confessionalism" is only half-way confessional, and the reason, again, is that the authors of the LBCF went beyond the Bible and imposed burdens that the Bible does not. To rely on that part of the LBCF to mandate local church membership is to lean on a broken reed. Jeff Durbin's accusations can easily turn against himself and make him culpable of the same (Matthew 7:2; Mark 4:24; and Luke 6:38). The only defense of the legitimacy of his ministry and church in that case is that they have fruit. But this, as we will see later, will also justify even those he intends to accuse.

3. The Anabaptism of Modern Presbyterians

I said above that the London Confession differs from the Westminster Confession in its view of mandatory "local church membership." There is more to it. The London Confession differs from *all* other Reformed confessions in this regard. No other Reformed confession includes mandatory "local church membership" as a religious obligation.

In fact, if we need to be even more general, this concept of "local church membership" never existed in the church before the 17th century. Yes, the concept of "church membership" has existed from the very beginning. The concept of "local congregation" has existed from the very beginning. The theology of "there is no salvation outside the church" has existed from the very beginning; hence, the command for Christians to "join the church" in a covenant, which is the Covenant of Grace. That joining the Church, though, was done through the same means a man joined the Covenant of Grace: baptism. Through baptism, man joined the *universal* Church. That is, the same Church mentioned in the Apostles' Creed, and then the Nicene Creed, and then in all the other great Creeds of Christendom:

> And I believe in one holy catholic and apostolic Church. I acknowledge one baptism for the remission of sins; . . .

The individual believer (or, "confessor," in the early centuries of the Church) automatically became in baptism a member of the universal Church, and through it, of all the "local congregations." He needed no additional oath, ceremony, or covenant to "join" a local congregation. Most people would stay within the same congregation, and some may even take voluntary vows of loyalty to each other: such is the way the first monasteries in Ireland and Scotland started. But such vows were never required for a believer to be considered a member or part of the church. A person could travel from place to place, join or attend or cooperate or worship with different Christian communities, or decide to remain for a long time alone, in the wilderness, or among heathens—and he was still part of the church. Now, we can have legitimate objections to asceticism, but this historical fact is incontrovertible: the early church highly valued ascetics. There is not a single line in the writings of the Church Fathers where ascetics were rejected because they "didn't join a local church." The Father of Orthodoxy, St. Athanasius himself, wrote a high praise of St. Anthony, for example. For all practical purposes, the early church was much more faithful to the principle of "by faith alone" than modern Reformed Baptists. One became a member of the Church by faith and creedal confession. Nothing else was needed. There may have been at times different stages of membership, but there has never been any such concept of "local membership." A member of the church in Jerusalem was also a member of the church in Corinth and a member of all the churches everywhere. Modern Baptists who claim that they just want to follow the early church, yet impose the LBCF's version of local church membership, are simply not being consistent.

The Reformation did not change anything in this regard. The Reformers worked to Christianize societies but they never mentioned anything about "local church membership." In the Geneva of Calvin, the city had a number of church buildings for church members to gather on Sunday (and every day, for that matter), but there was never a division of which family goes to which church, or any membership in a specific church. When there was a specific complaint against a person for his views (as against Servetus), that was taken before the whole Church, it was not an issue of a "local congregation" or a session. The Netherlands had city councils of elders but nothing remotely similar to "local churches." In Scotland, the very concept of a "national covenant" (hence the name "Covenanters") ruled out the idea of independent local congregations. In England, the community of the Independents was rather fluid, with itinerant preachers and "elders" being men of influence in the community rather than ecclesiastical hierarchy of "local churches." But membership was not assumed as a concept and not practiced by any church.

This universality of the Church was codified in the Confessions as well. As was said above, no other Reformed Confession ever laid the burden on believers to necessarily "join a local church." This is not to say that being part of the community of the Church (universal) and working together with other believers was not encouraged or commanded; but such bonding and working together was left to Christian liberty. Which means, all Reformed Confessions acknowledged that there were multiple ways in which a person could be part of the Church and work for and with other brethren without necessarily binding him to "join a local congregation." This includes the Westminster Confession, and the Savoy Declaration of 1658, a Congregationalist remake of the WCF. The most detailed of all, the Second Helvetic Confession (1566), specifically declared that the true Church extends beyond the visible Church, and therefore there may be members of the Church who are not part of the visible Church:

> Nevertheless, by the signs [of the true Church] mentioned above, we do not so narrowly restrict the Church as to teach that all those are outside the Church who either do not participate in the sacraments, at least not willingly and through contempt,

> but rather, being forced by necessity, unwillingly abstain from them or are deprived of them; or in whom faith sometimes fails, though it is not entirely extinguished and does not wholly cease; or in whom imperfections and errors due to weakness are found (Second Helvetic Confession, 1566, ch. 17).

This Confession continues covering the other end of the spectrum, namely, that not all who are in the visible churches are true members of the Church, and finally, ends with this warning:

> Hence we must be very careful not to judge before the time, nor undertake to exclude, reject or cut off those whom the Lord does not want to have excluded or rejected, and those whom we cannot eliminate without loss to the Church. On the other hand, we must be vigilant lest while the pious snore the wicked gain ground and do harm to the Church.
>
> Furthermore, we diligently teach that care is to be taken wherein the truth and unity of the Church chiefly lies, lest we rashly provoke and foster schisms in the Church. Unity consists not in outward rites and ceremonies, but rather in the truth and unity of the catholic faith. The catholic faith is not given to us by human laws, but by Holy Scriptures, of which the Apostles' Creed is a compendium. And, therefore, we read in the ancient writers that there was a manifold diversity of rites, but that they were free, and no one ever thought that the unity of the Church was thereby dissolved. So we teach that the true harmony of the Church consists in doctrines and in the true and harmonious

> preaching of the Gospel of Christ, and in rites that have been expressly delivered by the Lord. And here we especially urge that saying of the apostle: "Let those of us who are perfect have this mind; and if in any thing you are otherwise minded, God will reveal that also to you. Nevertheless let us walk by the same rule according to what we have attained, and let us be of the same mind" (Phil. 3:15 f.).

The background of this Confession—which was originally written as the personal confession of Heinrich Bullinger—is important to understanding the origin of the concept of mandatory "local church membership." It obviously did not come from the early church. It obviously did not come from the other Reformed traditions. In 1566, when Bullinger wrote the above lines, his main opponents were two groups coming from two opposite ends of the spectrum. At one end were the Papists, and at the other were Anabaptists. On the surface, they were opposed to each other. In reality, however, Papists and Anabaptists has similar views on the question of membership: it was that a true Christian must be part of the visible church. While for the papists the visible Church was the Roman priestocratic bureaucracy, for the Anabaptists it was their local "brotherhoods." Only membership in the local brotherhood made a person a true Anabaptist.

Now, I know that my Reformed Baptist brethren would respond that the real origin of modern Baptists is with the English Separatists. Fair enough, I don't disagree with this, when it comes to theology. *But when it comes to ecclesiology, and especially to the question of "local church membership," modern Baptists—and even modern Reformed Baptists—are closer to the Anabaptists and to other cultic sects.*

The first historical examples of making a covenant with a local community were indeed the Anabaptists in Germany and Switzerland. Membership in the community was the central characteristic, and the life of an Anabaptist had to revolve almost entirely around the local congregation. As early as 1527, the Hutterites, an early Anabaptist sect in Moravia, had an *Order of the Community: How a Christian Should Live* (*Ordnung der Gemein, wie ein Christ leben soll*) which tied the life of every believer to his local group. This *Ordnung* required that they met four or five times a week, and commit their lives and possessions to the local congregation for the needs of the congregation. The commitment was so severe that a special clause in the *Ordnung* required secrecy in relation to outsiders:

> What is officially judged among the brothers and sisters in the brotherhood shall not be made public before the world. The kind-hearted [an interested but not yet converted or committed] person shall be taught before he comes to the brothers in the brotherhood. When he has learned and has an earnest desire for it, and if he agrees to the essence of the Gospel, he shall be received by the Christian brotherhood as a brother or a sister, that is, as a fellow member of Christ. But this shall not be made public before the world to spare the conscience and for the sake of the purpose.

Mennonites practiced "local church membership" long before the English Baptists, and to this day, different modern Anabaptist groups do not acknowledge anyone to be one of them unless he has some sort of membership in a local congregation. The Membership Guidelines (2001) of the Mennonite Church USA, specifically acknowledge the right of the local congregation strictly to control local membership:

> Congregations have the authority to determine the criteria and the responsibility to implement the process for membership of persons joining their congregation, as well as leaving. They do so in con-

> sultation with their area conference and in consideration of expectations for membership in Mennonite Church USA ("Membership Guidelines," II:2).

The is another place the rules for local membership are very strict: the realm of the cults; and he further you move into that realm, the stricter the demand for local church membership gets. The Mormon Church has their strict rules for local church membership, as well as other quasi-Christian sects. For the sake of space, I will refrain from listing all the examples; the interested reader can verify this easily online.

One thing is perfectly clear: The more we move in the direction of historical, confessional, orthodox, creedal Christianity, the more the universal nature of the Church is emphasized (as in the Ecumenical Creeds), and the lower the standards for membership and participation in it. At the general level, baptism and public profession of faith are sufficient to make one a member of the Church—and by default, a member of any and every professing creedal orthodox congregation anywhere. There is no need for additional commitment to local bodies; such commitment is not sinful, but it is superfluous, and making it a requirement is anti-Biblical and anti-Confessional. On the other hand, the more we move in the direction of heterodoxy, heresies, and cults, the more the requirement for "local church membership" becomes mandatory, and the higher the standards for being a "member" of the church. In this, our Baptist brethren are straddling the fence: their theology is orthodox, but their ecclesiology on this point resembles that of the Anabaptist sects and the cults.

However, despite this ecclesiology being unbiblical, unorthodox, self-contradictory, and originating from the Anabaptist sects and being peculiar to all the pseudo-Christian cults, it can nevertheless claim victory in one thing: *today, most Reformed denominations and groups in the U.S. have adopted the same Anabaptist ecclesiology,* and the same non-Confessional standard of mandatory "local church membership." This Anabaptist ecclesiology is embedded in all the Books of Church Order of all the Presbyterian denominations in the U.S., contrary to any professed subscriptionism to the Westminster Confession, and contrary to the historical theology of Presbyterianism. The most inconsistent of all, of course, is the Communion of Reformed Evangelicals Churches (CREC), where many local congregations have an official theology of high-churchism and "Protestant catholicity" (also known as Federal Vision theology), but combined with extreme Anabaptist practices of mandatory "local church membership" and almost unlimited power for the local sessions over membership and over their flocks. Many include elaborate rituals of "local church covenant" and "admission into the local body." At the other end of the pipe, leaving a local church or transferring to another local church is often a huge issue of "authority" and power play, and such transfer of "membership" always involves special "permission" by the elders. There are dozens of cases within Presbyterian denominations in the U.S. where members of good standing have been *excommunicated* for daring move to another church, *even within the same denomination,* without permission from the local session. Presbyterian churches have all basically adopted the Mafia principle: "No one leaves us in good standing." Or, to stick to a theological interpretation, as far as ecclesiology is concerned, *modern Presbyterians are nothing more than Anabaptists.*

In none of the cases I have studied do modern Presbyterian leaders try to explain this departure from their own Confessional standards. In the few cases I have tried to engage some on this issue, their excuses have been two: *first,* that "without local church membership there will be no church discipline," and *second,* that mandatory "local church membership" falls under the "good and necessary consequence" clause in chapter 1, article 6 of the WCF. I will discuss the former when we get to the issue of church government and discipline. Of the latter, the "good and necessary consequence" clause has become to modern Presbyterian churchmen what the "general welfare" clause of the U.S. Constitution has become to modern liberals: an excuse to force onto the Confession a number of non-Confessional burdens. To make this point clear, and to see whether mandatory "local church membership" is really a "good and necessary consequence," the best course would be to check its validity against historical Presbyterian theology. If it is really a "good and necessary consequence," then early Presbyterian theologians would have taught it.

4. Presbyterian Theology Rejects Mandatory Membership

A study of historic Presbyterian theology, however, reveals that not only have Presbyterian theologians never taught such a thing, but they vehemently opposed the concept of mandatory "local church membership" whenever they encountered it. In fact, as we will see, some even opposed mandatory church membership in general, not just local, as false worship.

Calvin, spoke very strongly in favor of organized church communities; but not so strongly as to require that everyone be a member of one, no matter what its purity was. In his "anti-Nicodemite writings," he made it very clear that in the case where the churches in an area were all impure, the best course for a true Christian was to leave them and *worship in private*. Yes, *worship in private*! Here are Calvin's words:

> Some one will therefore ask me what counsel I would like to give to a believer who thus dwells in some Egypt or Babylon where he may not worship God purely, but is forced by the common practice to accommodate himself to bad things. The first advice would be to leave if he could.... If someone has no way to depart, I would counsel him to consider whether it would be possible for him to abstain from all idolatry in order to preserve himself pure and spotless toward God in both body and soul. *Then let him worship God in private, praying him to restore his poor church to its right estate ....*[4]

4. John Calvin, *Come Out From Among Them: The Anti-Nicodemite*

The early Presbyterian experience in Scotland in the second half of the 16th and the first half of the 17th centuries was rather chaotic. This was the time when the concept of the "national covenant" (hence the name "Covenanters") was opposed to the prelacy. In their strives against the prelacy, Covenanters sometimes took self-contradictory positions on different issues of ecclesiology. Some defended church hierarchy, others rejected it. Most operated (prophesied and taught) outside the visible institutional church. Some even rejected the necessity and the validity of ordination, even by their own fellow Covenanter elders, and yet were held in great esteem, and some even moderated General Assemblies (yes, while unordained). While a more detailed study of the Covenanters' ecclesiology in those early days of their work and doctrine should be a topic for another time, we can summarize their views as a healthy balance between serving the visible Church and acknowledging the service of the invisible Church. Serving the visible church was mandatory; the forms were left to Christian liberty. Joining a local congregation was highly desirable but *not* mandatory. Prophets should be under the discipline of the church, but when the visible church rejected them (like today's strict cessationist churches would do), they were free to operate outside her, and bring judgment on her. The majority of the early Scottish divines worked for certain periods of their lives outside any established church or congregation.

They could do that because in their view, the Church was not primarily the local churches but the universal body. It was this view of the Church that was encoded in the West minster Confession. I did not focus on the local churches but the universal Church.

Presbyterians first encountered the concept of mandatory "local church membership" in the 1630s, when Congregationalist preachers tried to establish a foothold in Scotland.

Writings of John Calvin (Protestant Heritage Press, 2001), 93–94; emphasis added.

The task of responding to it fell not to some minor Presbyterian preacher but to the Big Bertha of Covenanter theology, Samuel Rutherford. During the 1630s, Rutherford had been banished and cut off from the Church for his Presbyterian convictions; his only connection to the visible church at the time was his writing desk. If anyone fits the description of a "prophet outside the visible Church," or a "writing-desk prophet" (A "facebook prophet" of his day!) it would be Samuel Rutherford before 1638. He could have remained in the visible church during that time and obeyed the lawful authorities, but he refused. He could have organized his own local congregation, but he didn't. When Presbyterianism was reestablished in 1638, Rutherford returned to his ministry and took it upon himself to defend the ecclesiology of the Covenanters. He produced several books within the next decade. On ecclesiology in particular, his greatest contributions were *The Due Rights of Presbyteries* (1644) and *The Divine Right of Church Government and Excommunication* (1646). It is in *The Due Rights of Presbyteries* that he included his response against the localist ecclesiology of the Congregationalists.

The Congregationalist authors he took on had exactly the same views as modern Presbyterians and Baptists: a person is not a real believer unless he is a member of a local church, and unless he goes through what they called a "church covenant," that is, a specific commitment to a local body in addition to the general membership in the church through baptism. Rutherford strongly rejected the concept. He devoted over 60 pages (pp. 76–138) in a book of 450 pages total to oppose this error. His arguments are at times a bit wordy and hard to follow for a modern reader—he was, after all, trained in scholasticism—but we can mention his main points and conclusions.

First, Rutherford starts from the classical Calvinist affirmation of the superiority of the invisible Church over the visible Church. Which means, not all who are outside the visible Church are necessarily unbelievers. (This would make him and most of his predecessors and coworkers unbelievers for at least some periods of their lives, if it was true.) While joining a church is desirable, it is not mandatory, and has nothing to do with the covenantal status of a man before God. In his own words (quoting also from Augustine):

> There is a necessity of joyning our selves to a visible Church, but it is not *necessitas medii*, but *necessitas praecepti*, it is not such a necessity, as all are damned who are not within some visible Church, for Augustine is approved in this, "there be many Wolves within the Church, and many sheepe without"; but if God offer opportunity, all are obliged by God his Commandment of confessing Christ before men, to joyne themselves to the true visible Church.

Rutherford himself is rather ambiguous as to when and how this "opportunity" arises. He advises wisdom in leaving a church for being an unlawful assembly, or not fulfilling its obligations of a church, but in the final account, leaves it to Christian liberty, without any specific word of judgment.

Second, the manner of entering membership in the Church (universal) is through baptism and profession of faith. Nothing else is needed, no other commitments whatsoever. Commitment or covenant to a local church is allowed, not sinful, but *requiring* such covenant is unlawful. Rutherford's words:

> 1. Distinct. There is a covenant of free grace, betwixt God and sinners, founded upon the surety Christ Iesus; laid hold on by us, when we believe in Christ, but a Church Covenant differenced from this is in question, & sub judice lis est.

> 2. Distinct. There is a covenant of baptisme, made by all, and a covenant vertuall and implicite renewed, when we are to receive the Lords Supper, but an explicite positive professed Church covenant, by oath in-churching a person, or a society, to a State-church is now questioned.
>
> 3. Distinct. An explicite vocall Covenant whereby we bind our selves to the first three Articles in a tacite way, by entring in a new relation to such a Pastor, and to such a Flocke, we deny not, as if the thing were unlawfull for we may sweare to performe Gods commandements, observing all things requisite in a lawfull oath. 2. But that such a covenant is required by divine institution, as the essentiall forme of a Church and Church-membership, as though without this none were entered members of the visible Churches of the Apostles, nor can now be entered in Church-state, nor can have right unto the seales of the covenant, *we utterly deny.*[5]

He continues by showing that once a person has received baptism, he was by default a member of any congregation anywhere. There was no need for an additional covenant; if there was such a need, this would nullify the covenant in baptism.

Thus, *third,* he sees the requirement for local church covenant as an additional burden imposed on the believer's conscience, and therefore calls it "will-worship," or, in our modern language, "false worship." That is, any Presbyterian church today which practices such a requirement is in a

5. By the terms "Church-state" and "State-church," Rutherford does not mean a "government church," or "established church," but rather the "state of being in-churched," that is, the individual's position (state) of being a member of the church. This applies for later quotations as well where relevant.

direct violation of the Regulative Principle of Worship, according to Rutherford:

> All will-worship laying a band on the Conscience, where God hath layed none, is damnable; but to tye the oath of God to one particular duty rather then another, so as you cannot, without such an oath, enter into such a state, nor have title and right to the seales of grace and Gods Ordinances, is will-worship, and that by vertue of a divine Law, and is a binding of the Conscience where God hath not bound it.

Fourth, while the arguments he was addressing had come from Congregationalist authors, Rutherford correctly identified their real origin: the views of the Arminians and the Socinians, that is, the unorthodox sects. There is nothing Reformed in these mandatory "local church membership" arguments.

Was Rutherford alone in these views? Hardly. As I pointed out above, none of the Reformed Confessions required external membership in any particular body, and at least one emphasized the fact that believers not associated with any particular body are still members of the Church. A multitude of other Protestant divines could be cited here, but this would make this introductory booklet too long for its purpose. Thus, I will fast-forward to the second half of the 19th century to another prominent figure of Presbyterian theology, Charles Hodge.

Charles Hodge never lived through the trials and tribulations of Samuel Rutherford; he never had to operate outside the invisible church; he never had to be a "writing-desk prophet" with no congregation. He was the model Presbyterian theologian. It stands to reason, then, that he surely would have been much less willing to acknowledge the legitimacy of Christians without a visible body, and he would therefore have a much stricter view of the requirement of church membership, right?

Wrong.

In describing the church in his *Systematic Theology* (vol. I, pp. 134–139), he goes even further than Samuel Rutherford, not only openly declaring that the Church includes those who are not connected to any visible body, but also that *the very defining characteristic* of Protestant theology is this: the invisible Church over the visible Church. He repeats the same concept several times; obviously, he considered it very important. Here are Hodge's own words, when he describes "The Protestant Doctrine of the Church":

> (1.) That the Church as such, or in its essential nature, is not an external organization.

What follows from it is that membership in an external organization is *not* necessary:

> (2.) All true believers, in whom the Spirit of God dwells, are members of that Church which is the body of Christ, no matter with what ecclesiastical organization they may be connected, and *even although they have no such connection* [emphasis added].

In case we didn't get the message:

> (3.) Therefore, that the attributes, prerogatives, and promises of the Church do not belong to any external society as such, but to the true people of God collectively considered;

What does this mean in practice when membership in the Church is concerned?

> (4.) That the condition of membership in the true Church is not union with any organized society, but faith in Jesus Christ.

Even with this radical expression, he is not done. Consider the following paragraph:

> Protestants do not deny that there is a visible Church Catholic on earth, consisting of all those who profess the true religion, together with their children. But they are not all included in any one external society. They also admit that it is the duty of Christians to unite for the purpose of worship and mutual watch and care. They admit that to such associations and societies certain prerogatives and promises belong; that they have, or ought to have the officers whose qualifications and duties are prescribed in the Scriptures; that there always have been, and probably always will be, such Christian organizations, or visible churches. *But they deny that any one of these societies, or all of them collectively, constitute the Church for which Christ died*; in which He dwells by his Spirit; to which He has promised perpetuity, catholicity, unity, and divine guidance into the knowledge of the truth.

Notice how Charles Hodge is not even sure if such organized visible societies will always exist; he uses the word "probably": ". . . there always have been, and *probably* always will be, such . . . visible churches." Why "probably"? Because there is a deeper eschatology behind it, and we will talk about it later. Hodge continues in the same vein for several pages, supporting his case from the Reformed Confessions and from Reformed theologians, including Turretin. He comes to this conclusion about church membership:

> The doctrine that a man becomes a child of God and an heir of eternal life by membership in any external society, overturns the very foundations of the gospel, and introduces a new method of salvation.

That is, for Charles Hodge, the claim that the local church is "the most fundamental part of the life of a Christian," as well as the modern Presbyterian requirement of joining a local church, *are nothing more than plain Pelagian heresy.* Charles Hodge argues against the Romish church in these pages. But given that the same applied to the Anabaptists, he argues against all the heresies of salvation through works as well.

Between John Calvin, Samuel Rutherford and Charles Hodge, it should be very clear to any true Presbyterian deserving of the name which way Presbyterian theology goes. To this we can add A.A. Hodge: "A church has no right to make a condition of membership anything that Christ has not made a condition of salvation."[6] To this we can add a number of other Presbyterian theologians who made the difference between the invisible and the visible church a mark of Reformed theology, and therefore rejected the idea of mandatory connection to a visible body. Mandatory membership in the local church is not a Biblical requirement. Membership in a visible body was prescribed but not mandatory. If anything, it was an obligation of the church ministers to provide an opportunity by setting up churches. It was not the obligation of the individual member actively to seek out a church to join.

To close the circle of the true Presbyterian position, we only need to follow the practice of Presbyterian churches in the 19th century, during the same period when Charles Hodge taught and wrote his *Systematic Theology.*

We have evidence of those Presbyterian practices in the *History of the Presbyterian Church in America* by William

6. A.A. Hodge, *A Short History of Creeds and Confessions.*

Melanchton Glasgow, written in 1888. It is a rather long and detailed document, close to 800 pages, but what we are interested in is whether the Presbyterian church required membership in a visible body. There are multiple examples in the book that there was no such requirement, and a person was considered a member of the church even without being a member of a local body. Two quotations from the book will suffice:

> A few members have lived in the city of Chicago, and other localities, but no societies were ever organized.
>
> Waupaca. This city and vicinity were cultivated as a mission station by the Rev. James L. Pinkerton, in 1876, but no congregation was organized, as there were but a few families of Covenanters in that locality.

The *History* contains many more such examples, but the main point is obvious from just these two: one could be a Covenanter and a member of the church even without a local congregation. Reading more of the book, it becomes clear that the ministers of the Reformed Presbyterian Church considered it their obligation to create congregations, but there was no mandatory joining those congregations. In fact, according to the very founding documents of the Kirk of Scotland, it was much better to *not* have a church at all than to have a church lead by defective ministers:

> We are not ignorant that the rarity of godly and learned men shall seem to some a just reason why that so strait and sharp examination should not be taken universally; for so it shall appear that the most part of kirks shall have no minister at all. But let these men understand that the lack of able men

> shall not excuse us before God if, by our consent, unable men be placed over the flock of Christ Jesus; as also that, amongst the Gentiles, godly, learned men were also rare as they are now amongst us, when the apostle gave the same rule to try and examine ministers which we now follow. And last, let them understand that it is alike to have no minister at all, and to have an idol in the place of a true minister; yea and in some cases, it is worse. For those that are utterly destitute of ministers will be diligent to search for them; but those that have a vain shadow do commonly, without further care, content themselves with the same, and so they remain continually deceived, thinking that they have a minister, when in very deed they have none.[7]

Obviously, then, for Presbyterians in the past, being a member of a local church was not a priority. The priority was to have *able men* as ministers. In case there were no such men, it was actually considered better *not* to have a local church, and therefore no local church membership.

A few modern Presbyterians have tried to tell me their churches had "membership rolls" that go back 150 years, trying to prove that mandatory membership existed back then. The truth is, such "membership rolls" only prove that people joined those churches; they don't prove that such joining was *mandatory*. To the contrary, Glasgow's *History* clearly proves that the Presbyterian church in the 19th century agreed with Samuel Rutherford and Charles Hodge, that faith and public confession were the only necessary condition for being a member of the Church. Anything else was false worship and heresy.

---

7. *The First Book of Discipline* (1560). This book is largely the work of John Knox, "the Prophet and Apostle" of the Scottish nation, according to James Melville.

5. State-Imposed Ghettoization

Mandatory "local church membership" has never been part of the doctrine and the practices of the early church; it was never part of the Reformed doctrines; it was specifically rejected by Reformed Confessions and Reformed theologians. It came originally from Anabaptists and other sects. So the question is: Why did Reformed Baptists decide to differ from all the other Reformed groups on this point? Why did they go against the testimony of the Reformed faith and impose on their followers an unbiblical burden, creating such a logical conundrum?

Some would say, "Well, this is just Baptist theology and tradition, it separates us from everyone else."

Not really. This "Baptist theology and tradition" was not adopted by the earliest Baptists, but only later in 1689. The Confession of 1689 was the *Second* London Baptist Confession. There was a *First* London Baptist Confession, now largely ignored by the majority of Baptists. It was completed and adopted in 1644, two years before the Westminster Confession was completed and adopted. In theology, it didn't differ from the Second London Confession: it was Calvinist and Puritan to the core. In ecclesiology, however, it had some significant differences.

First, it mentioned no mandatory "local church membership" in any form. Local churches were mentioned, but no requirement for joining them. The focus was on the universal church.

Second, and more importantly, it did not define a church by having a government. That is, a church government was *not* necessary for the *being* of the church, only for its *well-be-*

ing. Here are the relevant lines in that Confession:

> XXXV.
>
> And all His servants are called thither, to present their bodies and souls, and to bring their gifts God has given them; so being come, they are here by Himself bestowed in their several order, peculiar place, due use, being fitly compact and knit together, according to the effectual working of every part, to the edification of itself in love.
>
> XXXVI.
>
> That being thus joined, every Church has power given them from Christ for their better well-being, to choose to themselves fitting persons into the office of Pastors, Teachers, Elders, Deacons, being qualified according to the Word, as those which Christ has appointed in His Testament, for the feeding, governing, serving, and building up of His Church, and that none other have to power to impose them, either these or any other.

Notice how the local church is expected to gather naturally, not by mandatory membership, and not needing any leadership for its existence. Only when it is gathered, for its *well-being*, it *has the power to* choose leaders, but it is not defined by having elders. Compare this to the 1689 Confession where the church itself is defined by a separation of classes between ministers and members.

Third, these church leaders, amazingly enough, are stripped of the monopoly of administering baptism—the opposite of the 1689 Confession in which the ministers are entrusted with the "peculiar administration of ordinances." The 1644 Confession says that this administration is not limited to officers:

XLI.

> The persons designed by Christ, to dispense this ordinance, the Scriptures hold forth to a preaching Disciple, it being no where tied to a particular church, officer, or person extraordinarily sent, the commission enjoining the administration, being given to them under no other consideration, but as considered Disciples.

Obviously, then, 1689 Baptists differed in their view of the Church not only from Presbyterians and Puritans and other Reformed. They also differed from the 1644 Baptists. Something changed between 1644 and 1689 to make Baptists switch from Reformed to Anabaptist ecclesiology. That something was not Reformed theology: as we saw, Reformed theology remained the same for another two centuries, at least. What changed it was a legislative shift in government policies.

It was, in fact, a 501(c)3 law. Or, a law that was similar to the modern 501(c)3 regulations in the US.

The return of Charles II to England in 1660 saw not only the restoration of the monarchy in England but also the re-establishment of the Church of England in a series of laws known as The Clarendon Code—the most important part of it being the Act of Uniformity of 1662. This Act of Uniformity regulated the relations between the government and the religious establishment, but it did so in a new way, different from anything prior. Prior to 1662, monarchs either tolerated different religious sects without any particular formal laws, at whim, or forced a form of religion on them. The Act of 1662 didn't *force* uniformity, it only precluded Non-Conformists from taking government positions, being teachers in schools, and earning degrees at Royal universities and colleges. They were also banned from having public meetings, although, private meetings were not banned. For this reason, it was also called the Non-Conformist Disabilities Act. The "uniformity" in the Act was *defensive,* not offensive. Baptist churches could exist now, it was just that their members suffered certain civil disabilities.

After the Glorious Revolution in 1688, William and Mary replaced the Act of Uniformity with a new act: the Act of Toleration of 1688. That act is very important to our study here.[8]

The Act of Toleration gave all dissenting Protestants (Non-Conformists) the right to free public worship, provided they took the oath of loyalty to the new sovereigns, King William and Queen Mary. The disabilities of the previous act were not repealed; Non-Conformists could still not take government positions, nor be teachers, nor go to royal colleges. These disabilities would remain for another two centuries; Charles Spurgeon, for examples, labored under them, and his support for the Liberals was based on their platform of repealing those disabilities. In all other respects, they were left alone, provided they took the oath of loyalty.

There were, however, Protestant Dissenters who did not want to take that oath either, and Baptists were among them. The Act had provided for these too: it required for every such minister who was a Protestant Dissenter at least two witnesses *and six members of his congregation* that he is indeed a Protestant Dissenter (and not, for example, Roman Catholic or non-Trinitarian). Here's the relevant text of the Act:

> XIV. Provided always, and be it enacted by the authority aforesaid, That in case any person shall refuse to take the said oaths, when tendered to them,

8. For the sake of brevity, I have only taken for analysis the main Reformed Baptist Confessions here. There were several General (that is, Arminian) Baptist Confessions, in 1611, 1655, etc., and there was a Statement of Orthodoxy (Reformed) in 1678 which was a precursor to the 1689 Confession. Very little in their content is relevant to this study, so I decided to leave them out, and keep them for future reference.

> which every justice of the peace is hereby empowered to do, such person shall not be admitted to make and subscribe the two declarations aforesaid, though required thereunto either before any justice of the peace, or at the general or quarter-sessions, before or after any conviction of popish recusancy, as aforesaid, unless such person can, within thirty one days after such tender of the declarations to him, produce two sufficient Protestant witnesses, to testify upon oath, that they believe him to be a Protestant dissenter, or a certificate under the hands of four Protestants, who are conformable to the Church of England, or have taken the oaths and subscribed the declaration above mentioned, and shall also produce a certificate under the hands and seals of six or more sufficient men of the congregation to which he belongs, owning him for one of them.

That is, *the Act granted toleration only where there was social visibility.*

This is a very important point in any study of the relations between the civil government and the church: *Rulers are afraid of the doctrine of the invisible Church, and of its practical applications.* Before 1688, most rulers in history had tried to suppress the invisible Church through persecutions and forced uniformity. The Toleration Act of 1688 was the first formal law passed by a European sovereign which tried to suppress the invisible Church through granting toleration for visibility. Or, as we call it today in our modern language, *incorporation*, that is, "in a [visible] body."

The Act, however, did something else as well: it *fragmented* the Christian community through local incorporation. The established Church of England was treated as a corporation without any special procedures for individual ministers. That is, any local Anglican vicar was officially acknowledged by the virtue of being part of the Church of England, whether he had any members of his congregation or not. The Act of Toleration required incorporation for every *individual* Non-Conformist minister, on the testimony of conformist Protestants and six or more members of his congregation. The churches now were allowed to exist only if, for government purposes, they registered separately of each other, and claimed each "member" separately for a specific individual church. There was to be no officially recognized universal body for Non-Conformists; only the state church had this privilege. The government would tolerate any free churches only as separate entities. Further, to register as separate entities, membership had to be membership *in* separate entities, "local churches." Ordination between churches did not count. The testimony of ministers from other Baptist churches did not count. Denominations did not count. Toleration was only granted where there was "local church membership."

The principle was the same as behind today's 501(c)3 regulations; the only difference was that instead of tax exemption, the ministers got toleration. For all practical purposes, the Act of Toleration was a 501(c)3 regulation. Or, for all practical purposes, the 501(c)3 regulation today is an Act of Toleration.

Baptist churches had been seeking such visibility and toleration under the restoration of Charles II, and they finally got it in 1688 after the Glorious Revolution. So now that they had it, they were prepared to have a Confession which encoded this official, but fragmented, visibility. No more universal Church, and no more theology of the "invisible Church." From now on, being a Baptist would entail participating visibly in the process of legitimizing your local Baptist community; if you did not, your pastor was in trouble with the authorities. This was an incentive which warranted including unbiblical burdens in the Confession. This was the reason why the Baptists in 1689 had to deviate so much in their ecclesiology from all the other groups, and from the Baptists of 1644.

While a study of the influence of 501(c)3 on modern ecclesiology goes beyond the scope of this booklet, it would still be relevant here to point out that the dominance of this Anabaptist ecclesiology in modern America coincided with the new Tolerance Act of 501(c)3. Just like in 1689, today, it pays for the individual churches to forsake the Reformation doctrine of the invisible church, and to go full visible, mandating "local church membership." The same practice of offering perks for visibility, incorporation, registration, etc. has been used by governments throughout history every time they had to deal with movements under the government's radar. Attempts at gun registration in the U.S. are one example of this practice; government aid to private schools or homeschooling families is another. In Eastern Europe in the 1980s, the Communist government started offering registration and legalizing of different dissident movements, with the purpose of drawing them into the open. In the 1970s and the 1980s, even Protestant churches were tolerated under Communism *if they were incorporated* (visible), while a simple prayer meeting behind locked doors could easily land the participants in prison. In all these cases, taking the government's bait has led to compromise and even betrayal of the ideology and the purpose of the movement. The Toleration Act of 1689 was such a bait, and the Reformed Baptists fell for it. For the next 200 years, they continued to exist in England, but their cultural influence waned. This influence had a short culmination in the ministry of Charles Spurgeon, who actually had to compromise on the question of membership in order to attract new attendees. After the removal of the disabilities, English Baptists never again played a notable part in the history of England.

6. The Eschatology of Self-Encapsulation

It is still true, though, that while the Reformed Baptists and a few other Non-Conformist groups abandoned the Reformed doctrine of the preeminence of the invisible Church, other Reformed groups did not. Presbyterians and others continued registering membership automatically upon baptism, with no requirement of an additional commitment to a local body. As I pointed out above, from William Glasgow's *History of the Reformed Presbyterian Church,* Presbyterian ministers considered as "members" people who had no local congregation of which to be members. They were obviously not so concerned about "submission to elders" and "church discipline" in this way. The concept of mandatory "local church membership" remained a characteristic only of the Baptist churches. While the political pressure for visibility of the local congregations broke the Baptists, it didn't break most others. This means that some other factor had to be at work as well.

That other factor was eschatology. Specifically, *pessimistic* eschatology.

In his major treatise on the rise and fall of civilizations, the British historian Arnold Toynbee made an interesting observation: that while a civilization has faith in the future and is expanding, it keeps open borders and builds its roads in a radial shape, from the center to the borders. Once it loses its optimism, it starts to encapsulate and focuses on building walls along its borders. The Roman Empire is a good example. In its years of expansion and optimism, it built very few defensive facilities—only walls of a few strategic cities. Once it reached what was considered the farthest possible limit of expansion, pessimism became the ruling sentiment about the future, and the Empire poured huge amounts of money into building gigantic defensive structures. Two still exist today in Britain, and there are remains of around 10 walls and dykes in Romania alone, of lengths between 30 and 100 miles, etc. Once a civilization or culture turns to fear of the future, it begins to encapsulate itself, even if previously it had no identifiable borders at all.

The same principle can be seen at work in the history of the United States. It is not a simple coincidence that the first anti-immigration laws were passed only after dispensationalism became the dominant eschatology in the American churches. Before 1921, Americans may have complained about this or that immigrant group, but the common perception was that the nation did not need closed borders. Obviously, an optimistic culture sees expansion as an inevitable destiny and a mandate, so borders are seen as an impediment. That is why the Declaration of Independence listed closed borders as one of the grievances against King George III. That is why the U.S. Constitution did not allow the Federal government to control immigration. That is why for four generations the U.S. had open borders for individuals who wanted to travel or to immigrate to it. Optimism needs no border control. It was only when a pessimistic eschatology was accepted in the churches, and a pessimistic ideology followed suit in the society and in politics, that a call for closed borders could be accepted as legitimate and supported by the population. In one of his lectures, R.J. Rushdoony also mentions the willingness of the Puritans and the Pilgrims in the colonies in New England to open their communities for outsiders, even criminals. Their optimism and faith in the power of Redemption to change people and societies gave them assurance that no danger of outsiders can be greater than the benefits that would flow from accepting and converting the newcomers. The Reformed Netherlands in the 16th and the

17th century had the same optimism and the same open borders for refugees from war-torn Germany, France, and Spain. In fact, during the 17th century, more than one-third of the population of the Netherlands was foreign-born.

The church followed the same policy of openness throughout the centuries. If we today, in our populated world, were to have a baptism service for 30 people, we would think it was a big event. Baptisms for hundreds and even thousands of people, however, were a normal thing in the age of early missions in Europe. From our modern perspective this sounds strange: How did they know every person, and how did they know he was a real convert? The truth is, *they didn't.* They didn't need to know. From the perspective of those early missionaries, people were not baptized into a local church—such a concept would mean absolutely nothing to the early church. These people were baptized into Jesus Christ, and thus into His universal Church; and through the universal Church, they were baptized into Christendom, that is, a comprehensive civilization that included everyone, including the false converts and even the unbelievers. Yes, many of these baptized people would know nothing of their new faith, and not all of them would be attending church. But the optimism of the early church told those early missionaries that no matter what happened after baptism, things were going to get better, and the society and the individuals in it would be growing in the faith, with or without churches or teachers. Yes, they worked to establish centers of learning and churches. But "the Church" was greater than the local congregations, and included all those who were baptized; and the Kingdom was even greater than the Church. So the churches kept their doors opened, and acknowledged as members of the Church all those who believed and professed Christ. For many centuries, a significant share of all Christians in the world were not under the direct "care" of ecclesiastical ministers. A growing civilization needs no such encapsulation.

It was only the cults who kept their ranks closed, and demanded strict rules for church membership and an extraordinary focus on submission to human authorities. The reason, again, was in part eschatological. Unlike the historic Church, cults and heresies never understood themselves to be bearers of a civilization the way the Church understood itself to be the bearer of Christendom. A cult is always busy separating itself from the world, it always views that separation from the world as so radical as to make it its defining characteristic. Cults and heresies, by denying one or another tenet of Trinitarianism, are by default dualistic. A dualistic religion is by default pessimistic about history and the world, because it does not have the presuppositional foundation to apply spiritual principles to the material world. Cults and heresies do not see the world as conquerable or as worth conquering; and therefore they do not expect to conquer it. They expect to remain small ghettos of the "true faith" against a world of growing darkness. Thus, building walls around those ghettos is mandatory. They need to separate clearly the insiders from the outsiders, often through a specific "covenant" of belonging, and often not just to a faith but also to a specific visible body.

In his book, *The Moral Imagination: The Art and Soul of Building Peace,*[9] the Mennonite scholar John Paul Lederach offers an extensive praise of pessimism as an attitude to life. In it, he connects pessimism to localism and insulation, to what he calls "proxemics," that is, "the study of the actual physical space that people view as necessary to set between themselves and others in order to feel comfortable." Pessimism makes people build walls around their communities and insulate themselves in small localities because the only positive change they can possibly perceive is local, limited to what their direct sense can perceive, or in Lederach's words, to "what can be *felt* and *touched*."[10] Pessimism thus makes

9. Oxford University Press, 2005, Ch. 6, "On the Gift of Pessimism."
10. Emphasis in original.

people lose a global perspective, for any global perspective is by default impossible to influence. Only local processes and changes can be influenced, and therefore only local processes and changes are worth paying attention to. Consequently, only people who make the local body the focus of their work and service are true public servants. A pessimist does not perceive any global processes; he can't even allow for their existence. When confronted with the reality of the universal church in the Confessions, he ignores the Confessions (even while he claims he subscribes to them) and asks his pessimistic question, "When is the last time you saw the universal church?" When shown the work and the service of men to the universal Church, he wants to see what they have done in some obscure small context—even if that obscure small community has never left any legacy of service to the universal Church. When given the facts about the historical growth of Christianity, his reply is always local: "Where can you see, with your own eyes, such growth?" A pessimist is always local, and therefore a pessimist always builds walls of separation between his community and the world. He does not expect his local body to conquer the world, so the battle becomes how to prevent the world from conquering his community, how to separate between the "faithful" and the "outsiders." This is where "local church membership" comes in as a convenient legal and psychological technique of building walls of separation against the world. All the faithful must come within these walls and remain there. Anyone who leaves the enclosure is leaving the faith.

The Bible, to the contrary, teaches optimism in history. With its optimism, it teaches a universal view which breaks all walls and encourages the faithful to break out of the mold and go out in the world. This teaching is everywhere in Scripture; in fact, one of the Old Testament promises about the New Covenant is that "Jerusalem will be inhabited without walls because of the multitude of men and cattle within it" (Zech. 2:4). The protection will be left to God, not to human devices, be they walls or "memberships." In the Bible, when the Kingdom of God operates, veils are torn, gates are broken and opened, and worship is freed from geographical and institutional constraints (John 4:21). Since he see global events to be subject to God, the Biblical optimist sees no reason to separate himself from them. The universal Church is more real to him than the supposed "local community," and wherever he joins a local group, it is only in the context of the greater purpose and work of the universal Church. He works locally but he is not limited to "local membership." The very concept of "local church membership" means nothing to him. The local church is not an independent covenantal agent to start with. It cannot make separate covenants for any kind of "membership." Given that the Biblical optimist expects victory in every area of life, he does not limit nor focus his gifts on one single area, local ecclesiastics. Such focus is a waste of resources to him, because the Kingdom is much larger than the Church, and certainly much larger than a local group which may or may not exist within a few years. His operational motto is, "Local churches come and go, the Kingdom remains forever." Or, to put it in the words of the Westminster Confession,

> The purest [local] Churches under heaven are subject both to mixture and error; and some have so degenerated, as to become no Churches of Christ, but synagogues of Satan. Nevertheless, there shall be always a Church on earth to worship God according to His will (WCF 25:5).

Thus, the Biblical optimist knows, reasonably deducted from his Bible and from the Confessions, his involvement with a local congregation must be reasonably limited. Many factors can influence such limitation of involvement: the significance of that local congregation in the larger picture of the Kingdom of God, the faithfulness of the people and the leadership of that local congregation to the Word of God, the nature and scope of his own gifts and calling, the realistic expectations for the future of that local gathering, etc. Long-term relational and economic investment, for example, in the church in Jerusalem before AD 70 would have been unreasonable, as would be the same in a local church in some mining town of declining population and no future. Also, for someone of the gifts and calling of Apostle Paul, undue commitment of time and effort and resources to some local gathering of Christians as over against commitment to the broader church community would be a gigantic waste of resources; imagine Paul in our modern "local churches" today, forced to change diapers in the nursery to prove he is a "true" Christian. For the pessimist, such consideration of the future and accounting of resources are useless; no effort of man has any meaning in the greater picture, because there is no greater picture to start with. An optimist first sees the greater picture; he first sees the future, not the current static conditions; and therefore his strategy is from the greater to the smaller, not the other way around.

Thus, it is not a surprise that mandatory "local church membership" became a dominant principle in the church in the 20th century, when pessimistic eschatologies like premillennialism and amillennialism made the Church abandon its commitment to expanding the Kingdom of Christ and replaced it with withdrawal from the world. Reformed Baptists lost that commitment as early as 1689. During the English Commonwealth, they were still carried along in the optimism of all the other Reformed groups. After the Restoration, Reformed Baptists never again thought of themselves as conquerors involved in building a new world order under Christ, or in mandating the moral, ideological, and social terms of the society. Even for the most optimistic of them, "victory" was not in changing history, but only in remaining faithful in their isolated communities against a hostile and powerful world. Even today, in any Baptist church, the history of the Baptists is told in terms of *survival* against all odds, not in terms of *conquest* against all odds. Even where Baptists were able to achieve numerical superiority against all the other faiths—as in the American South in the 20th century—they still did not create a dominant Christian culture.

It was puzzling to many of us in 2012 how and why Southern Baptists failed to support the only candidate who was professedly Baptist, had his profession of faith on the home page of his campaign website, and specifically related his political platform to the Bible: Ron Paul. They instead were trying to decide between one Roman Catholic and another Roman Catholic, both of whom supported, at one time or another Planned Parenthood. It is just as puzzling today how and why a judge in Alabama can be removed from his position for opposing abortion, by a panel of judges, most of whom are "members in good standing" of Baptist churches, and their churches do nothing about it. The answer is that these churches have that same pessimistic eschatology we talked about above, and therefore they can not see anything in the world outside their small ghettos. It is that same pessimism that helped bring about the concept of "local church membership": Whatever a man does outside the walls of the ghetto has no consequence. All that matters is what he does inside. The world outside the ghetto is unconquerable anyway, and there is no hope of building a Christian civilization or culture.

When the same ghetto eschatology was eventually adopted by the other branches of the Reformed family, the same concept of mandatory "local church membership" crept in as well. Where the eschatology of the church is optimistic, there are no walls of self-encapsulation.[11]

---

11. The same principle is at work in the conflict between the Christian culture of nuclear families versus pagan clan cultures: See Bojidar Marinov, "Christian Culture vs. Clan Culture." http://www.christendomrestored.com/blog/2012/11/christian-culture-vs-clan-culture/

7. God of Lone Rangers, Destroyer of Systems

Because of the optimism discussed in the last chapter, the Church in the past was not against, and certainly not afraid of, sending out Christians as "lone rangers," or of accepting them as a necessary part of its own growth. In fact, in the early centuries of the Church, Christian "lone rangers" were praised for their commitment and courage, and their lives were immortalized in official biographies. The literary genre of the biography or the autobiography was in fact very characteristic to the Christian culture—because it valued the individual person enough to make his life worthy of being recorded.[12] Moreover, of those whose lives were recorded and read in the early church—even as part of the worship service, at times—the vast majority were ascetics or lone missionaries.

There was a theological reason for this, and it had to do with the status of how man under God relates to society. Paganism has always been thoroughly collectivist and statist. It has always tried to bind the individual to a visible, organized collective. On this issue, Aristotle and Plato, despite their many differences, agreed: man needs a visible society to be man. Aristotle even denied human nature to those men who were "lone rangers," who didn't need any society:

> And why man is a social animal in a greater measure than any bee or any gregarious animal is clear.

12. Bojidar Marinov, "The Tale of the Two Aurelii: The Hero vs. the Real Man"; http://www.christendomrestored.com/blog/2012/08/the-tale-of-the-two-aurelii-the-hero-vs-the-real-man/

> . . . It is clear therefore that the state is also prior by nature to the individual; for if each individual when separate is not self-sufficient, he must be related to the whole state as other parts are to their whole, while a man who is incapable of entering into partnership, or who is so self-sufficing that he has no need to do so, is no part of a state, so that he must be either a beast or a god.[13]

Aristotle's words were accepted as normative throughout the world of Classical Greece and Rome. He based his argument on "natural law," and on the evidence from nature. Everyone just "saw" that man needs the collective to be truly man. Collectivism is thus inherent in paganism. The Classical world knew nothing of "lone rangers." Christianity, however, offered a different theology of man: *a man with God, even if alone against the whole world, is in the majority.*

We have some today who, imagining they are doing service to God, write diatribes against "lone rangers," throwing on them the blame for the failures of the church in the last century. But they are *actually* not serving God so much as the restoration of paganism and secularism, in all their collectivistic tyranny, distrust of self-control under God, and scorn of the individual who has a higher, transcendent calling, independent of man-made social engineering. Even when such men are sincere in their imaginations of the alleged danger of "lone rangers," they are still defending an anti-Christian worldview—a worldview that is self-destructive because it is unbiblical.

The simplest refutation of their position comes with the question: "What lone ranger can you name that has been a major factor for the failures and the decline of the church in the last one century?" None can be named. To the contrary, all the false doctrines in the church in the last one century, doctrines that have crippled the church and have made it

13. Aristotle, *Politics*, Book 1, 1253a.

passive and powerless and devoid of optimism—eschatological pessimism (premillennialism and amillennialism), pietism, antinomianism, statism, Arminianism, etc.—have been taught and promoted by *celebrities*. These are not lone rangers but men of enormous following, duly constituted local congregations, denominations, or seminaries.

Contrary to this, "lone rangers" have usually stayed busy trying to repair the damage done by these ecclesiastic celebrities. Among such "lone rangers" one can mention a number of names like R.J. Rushdoony, Arthur Pink, Leonard Ravenhill, and many more. Believing that "lone rangers" are by default dangerous to the Church while institutional churchmen are by default faithful Christians and leaders does not reveal a sound Christian mind; it only reveals an amazing blindness to the covenant realities of our age (not to mention previous ages, and the doctrine of total depravity in general).

It also reveals blindness to the realities of the Biblical message. In the Bible, the God we see is not a God of institutional systems. To the contrary, we see a God who destroys institutional systems when they prove to be in rebellion against Him. And guess what: *He often does so through independent individuals, through those same "lone rangers" so many Reformed and Reformed Baptist leaders today denounce as not being members of the Church.*

Are there "lone rangers" in the Bible? There certainly are, a whole host of them. We don't even have to mention Jesus, the Author of our faith, who stood alone against two systems, the Roman Empire and the Jewish religious leadership; we have many lesser men who were alone, and yet, with God, stood against systems and collectives.

We have Abraham, who was called out of his home and of his family to wander alone all his life. Yes, Abraham had his household but he was still called *alone*, according to Isaiah 51:2. God didn't call a congregation with elders out of Ur, He called *one* man, *alone*.

We have Moses, who was similarly called out of his people, and spent 40 years of his life alone among unbelievers, and then another 40 years alone in the wilderness. It was there, alone, in the wilderness, that God called him for his mission. Later, when he had the largest single congregation the world has ever seen, God still required Moses to come *alone* before Him when He delivered His Law (Ex. 24:2).

We have Elijah, of whom we never have a single record ever of submitting to any local congregation or elders, or serving a local body. ("Who are your elders, Elijah? Who santioned this behavior?") Amazingly, Jesus specifically underscores the fact that when Elijah helped a widow in her distress, it was a widow outside the covenanted body (Luke 4:26). Elijah spent much of his life alone, fed by ravens, or living in the house of a pagan widow, or on Mount Horeb, and yet, he continued prophesying against Israel. Ahab's complaint against Elijah echoes almost exactly our modern Baptist critics' complaints: "You, troubler of Israel" (1 Kings 18:17). An official leader of the covenanted community speaks in the name of the collective against a "lone ranger." *On whose side was God?*, is the relevant question here.

We can quote multiple other examples of "lone rangers" in the Old Testament, many summarized in Hebrews 11:38, and all praised for their faith:

> . . . men of whom the world was not worthy, wandering in deserts and mountains and caves and holes in the ground.

Do we have examples of unrighteous, wicked "lone rangers," people who stood against the visible covenanted community and its system of legitimate government just out of pride, not of love for God? We have at least one: Jeroboam (1 Kings 11–12). He rebelled against the rules of King Solomon and of his son, Rehoboam. We need to remember, King Solomon's rule was much more legitimate and lawfully established than the "leadership" of any modern Baptist or Presbyterian church; it was established directly by God, confirmed with prophecies and miracles. Modern Presbyterian and Baptist "churches" have nothing whatsoever to show to prove the legitimacy of their so-called "elders" except for the votes of other men, of whose legitimacy there is no proof either. *Yet, in this situation of one unrighteous "lone ranger" against a legitimately constituted authority over the covenanted community, God sided with the "lone ranger," and sent His prophets to encourage and support the "lone ranger."* This started as early as the reign of the Solomon (1 Kings 11:26-40).

We see the same thing in the New Testament. John the Baptist set the pattern, living alone in the wilderness, without submitting to any properly-constituted religious establishment. I have not read a single Baptist commentary explaining why a lone hermit outside all religious institutions and ordination could be a lawful authority to perform baptism and too call the established religious leadership of the day to repentance, or judgment! Presbyterian commentaries show the same deficiency. We see Jesus rebuking the disciples when they wanted to forbid a man from casting out demons (Mark 9:38–40; Luke 9:49–50). This Jesus-approved man was such a "lone ranger" that we don't even have his name recorded. We see a lone evangelist, Philip, baptizing an Ethiopian (Acts 8) who returned to his country, and had to have been the only Christian there, given that Ethiopians were not mentioned among the converts in Acts 2.

The Apostle Paul is not usually thought of as a "lone ranger," but the testimony of the Book of Acts and some of his own epistles give us enough indication that he was a man of independent spirit and, when necessary, thought very little of official organizational structures. Before he went on his first missionary journey, there was some sort of laying of hands by the prophets and teachers (no "elders" or "overseers" mentioned here) in Antioch (Acts 13:1–3), and yet, the text clearly emphasizes the fact that the sending was done by the Holy Spirit Himself. Paul himself never referred to the church in Antioch as his "congregation" or "sending church." He never mentioned his ordination by men. The questions so cherished by modern ecclesiocrats—"Who are your elders?" "Are you in submission to elders?"—seem to be ignored completely by Paul. If anything, Paul insisted to the Galatians that he was ordained and sent not by men (Gal. 1:1). It is to these same Galatians (2:11–21) that Paul related the incident in Antioch, in the very church that laid hands on him and sent him out, to which church Paul should have submitted, if he obeyed our modern mythologies of submission to the local church.

Keep in mind that by the time of that incident, Paul was still not the authority he is today. He had finished only one missionary journey—not an overwhelming feat, for many others had done missions, too. He had just returned from the Council in Jerusalem which approved of his work, but remember, at that Council, *Paul was not a participating apostle but a defendant.* The Council was a church court, and Paul was examined for the orthodoxy of his ideas and practices. One of his judges was Peter himself. A few weeks or months later, the two met in the church in Antioch, where Paul dared challenge Peter for his practices and views. Remember, Paul was still nobody compared to the Chief of the Apostles. Few, if any in the church supported Paul's views; the text clearly says that the rest of the Jews and even his beloved Barnabas joined Peter in his hypocrisy. It was a clear position of the majority in the church: the Chief of the Apostles, the elders and the members of the church, and even Paul's closest associates.

Nothing in our modern churchian mythologies of "submission" and "local church membership" can explain Paul's actions when he saw that hypocrisy. The man who just recently was a *defendant* in a church court, a nobody compared to many of the elder statesmen. Paul was alone against the whole church, opposed the Chief of the Apostles "to his face" and accused him of hypocrisy, and of nullifying the grace of God and of the sacrifice of Christ. Yes, this relatively recent convert, spoke to the face of the Apostle who personally saw Christ, lived with Christ, and received personally Christ's last testament to care for His Church (John 21:15–17).

We do not know Peter's immediate response. We know he eventually agreed with Paul. In his second epistle, written 10–15 years later, he spoke well of Paul and his writings (1 Pet. 3:15). Whatever his response may have been at that moment, there is a lesson here for today's critics: even if a "lone ranger" opposed them to their faces, in their own churches, in front of everyone, they had better not be quick to dismiss that man, for they may be dismissing God Himself. Bear this in mind before dismissing "Facebook prophets" so harshly. Until we learn the same humility and submission as Peter—to accept true correction no matter where it comes from—we are unqualified to tell others how to submit.

There is an even greater lesson in all these examples of "lone rangers" in the Bible: God almost never speaks or gives prophetic word through established church hierarchies. He usually prefers to speak through lone individuals. When a covenanted organization faces a lone individual who denounces the organization or calls it to repentance, odds are, God is the one who raised that lone individual (1 Kings 11), and the formal legitimacy of the organization is of little consequence to God and to His covenant. Anyone who denounces prophets or adversaries solely on the basis of their lack of "local church membership," therefore, or because they are "lone rangers," is not Biblically justified. Paul had a good reason to say, "Do not despise prophecies" (1 Thess. 5:20). God is a God of "lone rangers," and a Destroyer of man-made systems.

8. The Modern Mythologies of "Submission," "Accountability," and "Church Discipline"

There is not, and never has been, any Biblical argument in favor of mandatory "local church membership." The Bible just does not mention it. In fact, it clearly indicates that God supports individuals against collectives more often than He supports collectives against individuals; for one reason or another, men in collectives are much more tempted to stand against Him than men who are alone. Because there is no Biblical argument for mandatory "local church membership," modern churchmen resort to a rationalist argument: "Without local church membership, there can be no submission to elders, no accountability, and no church discipline."

This fact needs to be emphasized: no matter how popular this argument is today among modern ecclesiocrats, no matter how often they use it in their sermons and lectures and writings, *the argument is not Biblical*: it cannot be found in the Bible, and it cannot be reasonably derived from any Biblical teaching whatsoever, for it clearly contradicts the Biblical evidence. Submission, accountability, and church discipline in the Bible were clearly done without an additional covenant or any other additional burden related to "local church membership."

A presuppositional analysis of the argument shows clearly that it is a rationalist argument, not a Biblical argument. It starts with an a priori definition of "submission" as "submission *to the local church*," of "accountability" as "accountability *to the local church,*" and "discipline" as "discipline *by the local church.*" Once the local church has been included as a necessary condition in the very definitions of these things, then, of course, the question is asked, "How do you have submission, accountability, or discipline without the local church?"

This tactic is the same as the propaganda trick used by socialists today: their definitions of "welfare" and "charity" include mandatory redistribution of wealth as a necessary condition, so their answer to any free market solution is, "How will we have charity if the government doesn't tax the rich?" Roads, of course, are always by definition built by the government; private entities cannot build roads, therefore, "Who's gonna build the roads?" Education is by default government education, so when we call for the abolition of government schools, the answer is, "How would people get education then?" Examples of such propaganda manipulation are everywhere around us. In the same way, the modern churchian leaders, after they have redefined "submission," "accountability," and "discipline," ask the same manipulative propaganda question: "Without local church membership, how can we have submission, accountability, or discipline?"

Yet when we look at the results in the American church over the last century, after the doctrine of "local church membership" became dominant, we do not see the claimed results. Not only are discipline and accountability at an all-time low, but the church in America has been losing the cultural war for three generations in a row. Whatever the churchmen imagine about the value of their "local church membership," it apparently contributes nothing to the strength of the church. Baptists, of course, have always been widely varied theologically and practically. As early as the 1640s, there were several Baptist confessions in England, some Calvinist, some extreme Arminian. The 19th century continued the same divide, and there were spin-offs from the two main branches that went into many heretical ideologies. Even today, there is no unified view among Baptists, even within the same denomination. Just recently, a high-level celebrity within the Southern Baptist Convention called for the excommunication of all the Calvinists from the Convention. As if that was not enough, another celebrity-status pastor recently declared that one's salvation is dependent on voting for Donald Trump. It took the SBC more than 50 years after the beginning of the Christian homeschool movement to come to some sort of unified, although still unclear, position on who should be teaching the children of Christian parents. Some churches in the denomination have accepted sodomite marriage. One would think that this is where at least Baptists would draw the line, but no. The situation is even worse when one looks at more than just the SBC, and when one looks at more than just theological and practical views.

No matter how one tries to twist the evidence, the truth is, Baptists, who have had a confessional requirement for mandatory "local church membership" for three and a half centuries, have, of all the major Protestant groups, the worst possible record of accountability and church discipline.

The other groups and denominations—Presbyterians, Episcopalians (Anglican), Methodists, Dutch Reformed, Hungarian Reformed, Lutheran—have not had such confessional requirement, and while there have been splits and problems, all of them together could not rival the theological and ideological chaos within the Baptist movement . . . *until the 20th century*, when all these groups also accepted the Baptist ideology of ghettoization of the church. And, guess what, it led to the same result as with the Baptists: not only numerous splits, but also a proliferation of anti-Biblical ideologies within their churches. This includes hundreds of cases of scandalous behavior and practices, and outright betrayal of basic principles of the Gospel which remain not only unpunished, but in some cases are encoded as normative in the very constitutions of some churches.[14]

14. See, for example, Edmund W. Robb and Julia Robb, *The Betray-*

In the face of the overwhelming historical and current evidence, *it is difficult to see how any person can seriously claim that mandatory "local church membership" is necessary for maintaining accountability and discipline in the church.* Such reasoning, however, is common in the American church today because these terms have not been taken in their Biblical meaning. *They have rather been developed into a modern mythology*—a mythology designed to solidify the power of the churchian elites over the mass of ordinary Christians.

From R. J. Rushdoony's extensive studies on the sociological and political implications of paganism and Christian theism (that is, trinitarianism),[15] we know that all pagan mythologies, religions, and ideologies are by default statist and collectivist. We also saw Aristotle's declaration that one who does not fit in a society is not even a human. There is a good reason for such collectivism: *paganism has a problem with the issue of unity.* If there is not a transcendent Creator-God of the world (polytheism or atheism), or if that God is silent (Islam or Arianism), or if that God is silent on the current applications of His Word (modern cessationism—baptized rationalism),[16] then there can be no *transcendent* principle of cohesion between men in the society. Or, at the very least, such principle would be impossible to know and comprehend. If there is no such principle, it is left to *human agencies* to provide it for individuals in the society. If there *is* such a principle, it will be so concealed that only an "enlightened" or "spiritual" elite would be able to decipher it and convey it to all—which is, again, human agencies providing cohesion

---

al of the Church.

15. See *The One and the Many: Studies in the Philosophy of Order and Ultimacy* and *The Foundations of Social Order: Studies in the Creeds and Councils of the Early Church.* See also Numa Denis Fustel De Coulanges, *The Ancient City: A Study on the Religion, Laws, and Institutions of Greece and Rome*; Charles Norris Cochrane, *Christianity and Classical Culture: A Study of Thought and Action from Augustus to Augustine.*

16. R. J. Rushdoony, *Systematic Theology,* vol. 1, pp. 296, 323–26.

and unity. No matter what the starting point of a society's thinking is, if it is not consistent Trinitarianism (equal ultimacy of unity and plurality, of transcendence and immanence), that society will tend to degenerate into some sort of collectivism. In the final account, an elite—educational, religious, military, political—will take over in an attempt to provide the unity in that society. This is why all pagan religions and ideologies inevitably produce collectivist and totalitarian societies and cultures.

Once the issue of unity is thus placed in the hands of an elite, of a human agency, then that human agency must be declared divine (or at least invested with exclusive divine authority), for no challenge to its power can be tolerated. The issue, note well, is not just political or organizational; *it is first and foremost religious*. Belonging to the collective, submitting to its elite (elders, leaders, commanders, or whatever you name it) becomes now a "fundamental part of the life" of the member of the society. It is "God's design" for him. His refusal to submit absolutely "under the care" of his official leaders by default means that he "despises authority," for not being "under the care" of the elite means that a man despises the official unity—as defined by the elite. (Remember, there is no unity except for what the elite provides.) Thus, in all paganism, the individual is always viewed with suspicion and distrust; "lone rangers" are always expected to be "troublemakers," destroyers of that divine unity and cohesion provided by the elite. All social theory and practice of paganism—or of that deficient Christianity which practically deifies the collective—therefore has for its goal the subjection of the individual and the automatic placement of the elite themselves above judgment, accountability, above discipline. Unless the "leaders" are free of accountability, there can be no protection against the "danger" of free men who exercise their private judgment.

This special privilege is the very purpose of the modern mythologies of "submission," "accountability," or "church discipline." They always speak of "submission, accountability, and discipline" for individuals. *They rarely if ever speak of "submission, accountability, and discipline" for church sessions.* There is hardly a word in all their writings and speaking of what the obligations and limits of church sessions are—and therefore of what the *punishments* for church sessions are when they violate their obligations. There is rarely if ever direction for resisting or opposing elders or sessions who exceed their authority. There are, in fact, sometimes specific guidelines that protect local church sessions or elders from any higher authority or accountability.

One of my elders in the past, involved in planting a church with other elders, sat through a meeting listening to them talk about different spheres of government—family, church, and state—about their rights and responsibilities, and about the Biblical principles of mutual control between these levels of government. For example, what can the church speak to the government in terms of correction, to the family, etc.? At some point in the discussion, he asked, "Aren't we missing one level of government, the most important one? What about *self-government,* its responsibilities, and its rights to correct and discipline the other governments?" The "session" went silent for a moment, then ignored his words, and continued as if he had said nothing.

I wish this type of problem existed in just one church session, but it does not. There is not a single Book of Church Order in any church or denomination in the U.S. today which acknowledges the rights and responsibilities of self-government, and allows it certain power and privileges over church government. Self-government does not exist; or, if it exists, it is only pro-forma, in the form of "submission" to the "local church." You have to submit to the local church, otherwise you don't have "self-government." The question is, of course, "Submit to what? What are you going to ask me to do?" But that answer is left vague and undefined in the books of the modern ecclesiocrats.

Under these modern mythologies, there is never the question of accountability or discipline for a local session. Who is you favorite Baptist pastor accountable to? Just to his session which probably consists of his handpicked closest friends? If this is "accountability," then anyone can claim "accountability" to his buddies. Who can excommunicate that pastor and his session if they commit injustice as a session within their church? Is such accountability included in the church's constitution? Does it say who can excommunicate the session if they commit injustice?

Back in the 1980s, cops from the LAPD's SWAT team tortured activists of Operation Rescue on the streets of Los Angeles; they also kicked a pregnant mother until they killed her unborn baby. The cops were led by Bob Vernon, who was also an elder in John MacArthur's church. Vernon sought and received the full support of his "local church leadership," and later, John MacArthur even held a special service to honor the same cops who had brutalized other Christians and had murdered an unborn baby. No repentance came out from either Vernon or MacArthur's church elders, not even a formal apology. Who holds MacArthur responsible for supporting this? Who can take MacArthur to a church court and excommunicate him if found guilty? Reformed Baptist and other Reformed leaders all over call MacArthur a hero of the faith. Does this mean that some day, if for one reason or another, their own sessions or elders were to sanction such a crime, there will be no accountability for them either?

Yes, that is what it means. That is the very purpose of the modern mythologies of "submission," "accountability," and "church discipline": it robs individual Christians of their Christian liberty and establishes the power of churchian elites over the individual conscience of their members. It frees the churchian celebrities of our age of accountability and makes then invulnerable to discipline. As I pointed in my article on "Modern Presbyterianism and the Destruction of the Principle of Plurality of Elders,"[17] no matter what decision a church session makes, there is no punishment, no accountability, no discipline. As long as an elder does not go "rogue," that is, does not go against the collective of other elders, he can commit virtually any kind of injustice, and get away with it. This is not limited to Presbyterianism; it applies to nearly every single session of every single church or denomination in the U.S.

The only possible solution to this problem of the lack of accountability and discipline for churchian celebrities and elites is when individual people start leaving their churches, realizing the corruption of such so-called "elders" and their so-called "sessions." Since there is no accountability for the very leaders who demand accountability, and since there is no discipline for the same people who claim to enforce discipline, then the individual members of their flocks who want to remain faithful to Christ and His true Church would have only one resort: leave, and take their money with them. Quit supporting fake, corrupt, or compromised leaders. Perhaps even take their money to the true prophets and teachers of God, who have not bowed their knees to Baal. Like that man of Baal-Shalisha (literally meaning the "Lord of the Trinity") in 2 Kings 4:42, who, instead of bringing the bread of his first fruits to the Temple as the Law required (Ex. 23:19), brought it to Elisha, the Prophet of God. Elisha did not return him to the Temple, but used the bread to perform a miracle, multiplying bread for a multitude of people. Apparently, God was quite pleased that the man did not obey His Law in the technical and ceremonial detail, but obeyed it in its spirit. And if the Temple that was established personally by God did not deserve the first fruits because its leadership was corrupt, why should modern "local churches" who have proven to be fake and useless deserve any better?

---

17. http://www.christendomrestored.com/blog/2016/02/modern-presbyterianism-and-the-destruction-of-the-principle-of-plurality-of-elders/

At this point, the doctrine of the mandatory "local church membership" comes to play its most important role: not to secure accountability and discipline, but to ensnare the loyalty of individual Christians. Because, you know, unless you are a "member," and give your tithe to a "church" without holding them accountable, you are not a true Christian. If you were to desire to hold them accountable, do not forget you are a member: you have made a covenant to submit, and they can "excommunicate" you, while you have no recourse against their decision. This has nothing to do with real discipline and real accountability. The doctrine is specifically made to protect the elites. R. J. Rushdoony said, commenting on the local church, "The attitude of the modern man is that status is a license for irresponsibility."[18] That attitude has become encoded in the mythologies of "submission," "accountability," and "church discipline."

That is one *big* reason the church has been in such a sorry state for at least the last 100 years.

18. *Systematic Theology*, Vol. II, p. 685.

9. Submission to Church Bureaucrats is Not in the Bible

The mythology of "submission to elders" needs special attention given that it has become the main objection to the universal view of the church encoded in the Confessions. It is a mantra of the modern church that millions of Christians have accepted as true by default without checking their Bible, like true Bereans, to see if the Bible really supports such a concept.

The behvaior of these modern church tyrants stems from a unbiblical view of power and submission. A full analysis of this theory of power and submission to power would take too much space for thsi introductory work, so I will constrain myself to a summary while adding only that several such theories supporting different sorts of collectivisms have raised their heads in the Church today: establishmentarianism, patriarchalism, high-churchism etc. Suffice to say here that such theory of power and submission is not based on the Bible and is not supported by the covenantal worldview of the Bible. It is based rather on "natural law" theory. Under "natural law" theory, "naturally" existing power must be necessarily exercised, or it is wasted. A person in power is supposed to exercise his power to force others to do good, not let it lie passively and only use it to prevent them from doing evil. The father in the family (as the most powerful person in the family), the ruler in civil government (as the most powerful person in a geographical territory), or the session of elders in the church (as those who wield the power of ultimate decisions in the church) would be wasting the power given to them if they do not use it to make individuals follow their agenda. Likewise, individuals would be "disrespecting authority" if they rely on their individual judgment and maturity, if they follow their own agenda, vision, and mission—especially if that individual agenda and vision and mission is not approved by the powerful of the day. This, again, will be left for another time. For now, it is enough to remember that modern statism did not appear out of nothing. It was modeled after modern church collectivism, or the same doctrine of "submission to elders" that is so popular today in our churches.

The Biblical doctrine of power and submission is exactly the opposite to that of "natural law." The Law of God clearly limits the extent of all power in the society and leaves the greatest power to *self-government*. The New Testament supports this "rugged individualism" of the Law by declaring that "the head of every man is Christ" (1 Cor. 11:3). Not his pastor or elders, nor his civil government. In addition, Jesus specifically declared that in His Kingdom, the pagan order of hierarchy—from the powerful to the weak—is turned on its head, and it is those who serve that are the true authority, not those of power:

> And there arose also a dispute among them *as to* which one of them was regarded to be greatest. And He said to them, "The kings of the Gentiles lord it over them; and those who have authority over them are called 'Benefactors.' But *it is* not this way with you, but the one who is the greatest among you must become like the youngest, and the leader like the servant. For who is greater, the one who reclines *at the table* or the one who serves? Is it not the one who reclines *at the table?* But I am among you as the one who serves" (Luke 22:24–27).

In the Kingdom of God, legal, physical, intellectual, governmental, or ecclesiastical power is not the basis for authority. The opposite is true: the less a man uses his power to lord over other people and the more he uses is to serve (as the one who serves at the table), the higher his true authority is. This reversed system of power versus authority is apparently very important, given that Jesus repeats the same principle multiple times (Matt. 20:25–28; 23:11; Mark 9:35–37; 10:42–45; Luke 9:46–48; etc.).

Moreover, the more power a man is given, the more he must be held accountable and the worse the punishments he should receive in case he commits transgression (Luke 12:48). The men who are given greater power in the church—or in any society—should not also be given blind submission, for this would express a pagan order. To the contrary, they must be held to the strictest standards, under severe control, constantly supervised, and immediately punished and sacked in case of transgression. *Only in a pagan social order is submission given to men in power. In a covenantal society, submission should be given to servants.* Servants are given all the freedom they need to work and serve. Powerful men are kept on a short leash and immediately rebelled against and punished when they cross their lines.

Thus, contrary to all the modern mythologies of some "biblical command" to submit to elders in the sense of church bureaucrats, the Bible contains no such command. It certainly contains commandments to submit to *authority*, but, following Jesus's statement quoted above, that authority has nothing to do with legal power or structures in the churches.

To start with, the only verse that specifically says "submit to your elders" in the English translation, clearly doesn't have "elders" as "church leaders":

> You younger men, likewise, be subject to *your* elders (1 Peter 5:5).

The clear meaning of the word "elders" is the original, direct meaning: "older men." (That is the meaning of the word *presbus* in Greek.) The counterpoint between *older* (*presbuteros*) and *younger* (*neoteros*) is the same as in 1 Timothy 5:1: "Do not sharply rebuke an older man, but rather appeal to him as a father, to the younger men as brothers."

Some may object that Peter had in mind *church* elders, given that the context in the first four verses of 1 Peter 5 indicates men in formal office. Such formal office, however, has to be assumed first and then read into these verses; even then, it is not clear why only the *younger* ones are admonished to obey. Are the older non-elders not commanded to obey?

The more Biblical interpretation of the word "elders" in Peter's words is not "church administrators" but "men of authority," whether these men had any official judicial power in the church or not. The same Greek word of "be subject" (*hupotasso*) is applied in other places for different circumstances, but an important one in respect to "submit" is 1 Corinthians 16:16, where Paul commands the church at Corinth to "be in subjection to such," and from the previous verse the "such" are the "household of Stephanas." Obviously, the whole "household" can not be a group of church administrators, for the word includes also the women in the household (and, if you are a paedobaptist, the children as well). The special position of authority of Stephanas's household was that they "were the first fruits of Achaia, and have devoted themselves for ministry to the saints." Their authority for receiving submission just like "elders"—older in the faith than anyone else in that church—had nothing to do with their position of legal power but with their *service*. That is, just as Jesus said it should be: it is the servants who should be rendered submission, not the rulers. For this reason, immediately after directing the Corinthians to submit to this family, Paul adds that this applies also "to everyone who helps in the work and labors." Obviously, submission is due to those who serve.

The same focus on submission for service is in Hebrews 13:17: "Obey your leaders and submit to them, for they keep watch over your souls as those who will give an account." Again, the assumption that the "leaders" here are "church officers" is unwarranted. The description could fit anyone in a position of teaching, influence, and authority—church bureaucrats or not. It would, in fact, exclude any "church elders" who can not demonstrate responsibility for another's soul. Such deserve no obedience and submission whatsoever, no matter what their official title in the church is.

This point is further emphasized in 1 Timothy 5:17:

> The elders who rule well are to be considered worthy of double honor, especially those who work hard at preaching and teaching.

This is the closest statement in the Bible of obedience—or rather, "double honor"—to church officers, for the designation "elder" is clearly connected to the word "rule." Yet, even here, "double honor" is *only conditional*: "the elders *who rule well*." If we assume this verse speaks of church officers, the question we need to ask is, *Who decides which elders rule well and which do not*? Do we let the church officers say so themselves? We already know the standard for good rule: service. *But who or what institution decides if an elder really lives up to that standard*?

To answer this question, we need to raise from oblivion one of the most important, and yet the most forgotten, doctrines of the Reformation—a doctrine that in previous centuries was understood to be the very mark of Protestantism itself by almost every Reformed theologian, yet today is rarely mentioned by any. In the few places where it is mentioned, it is only to be rejected, maligned, and ridiculed. What doctrine is this? It is the doctrine of *the right and duty of private judgment.*

10. The Priesthood of All Believers and the Right and Duty of Private Judgment

What is missing from the mythologies of the modern church is one of the foundational doctrines of the Reformation: *the priesthood of all believers*. No, it is not that the modern "Reformed" preachers and even celebrities do not mention that doctrine. Rather, the way they teach it is vastly different from what the Reformers meant.

A number of examples could be presented of the modern, twisted meaning of this doctrine, but one article by Ligonier Ministries makes a representative example: "A Royal Priesthood in Christ." Going to the Old Testament for the meaning of our priesthood, the article ends with the following summary:

> In Christ, there is a true priesthood of all believers. All of us who trust in Jesus alone for salvation have free access into His presence, and all of our lawful vocations are set apart for true God-honoring service.

Notice how the "priesthood" is limited: it is restricted to our *access* to God and to our *salvation*. That is, our priesthood is limited to our *passive standing* before God, and perhaps to our daily job routine as well. This is entirely in agreement with the modern mythologies of "submission" we discussed. Whatever we do as individuals and priests, we do not have any authority above and beyond our own personal life and salvation. Our "priesthood" only counts for our salvation. Nothing else.

But the author of this Ligonier article is incorrect: this is not what the function of the priesthood was in the Old Testament, and this is not what the Reformers had in mind when they proclaimed the priesthood of all believers. A priest was not simply one who *was personally saved* by having direct access to God. The concept of priesthood was a concept of mediatorial service, and of *judiciary authority* in the name of God and based on His Law. It was not the direct access to God that defined a priest—in fact, only one priest could actually enter the Holy of Holies once a year. (If anyone had direct access to God all the time, it seems to have been the prophets, not the priests.) People were certainly saved without being priests—saved directly by God. People could give offerings to God without a priest, or could make their offering to non-priests (2 Kings 4:42). Non-priests could enter the Temple and eat of the bread that was ceremonially reserved for the priests. The function of the priests was to read the Law and to interpret it to other people. It was not their status before God that defined them as priests; it was their function to the world outside the Temple and even outside the covenanted community that defined them as priests. They were supposed to read the Word, and *judge* everything based on their understanding of the Word.[19] Yes, judge even the church and the other priests of the covenanted community.

Thus we come to one of the most puzzling mysteries of modern Protestantism: *the complete disappearance of the doctrine of the right and duty of private judgment from our modern pulpits.*

It was part of Luther's idea of the priesthood of all believers that every believer is entitled to his *private judgment* as to what the Word of God says, and is, in fact, *obligated* to exercise his *private judgment* in relation to whatever the

19. See *Axe to the Root Podcast*, "Covenantal Thinking." http://reconstructionistradio.com/axe-to-the-root-covenantal-thinking/

church or the civil authorities say. Any submission to any kind of authority must start from the personal conscience of the individual, and therefore from his private judgment. There was more to Luther's idea: the priesthood of all believers made it the rule that any Christian has the mandate to preach the Word of God to any authorities and to any audience, whether he has a permission from bishops or popes or not.[20] Submission to authorities, in Luther's view, was to be *conditional,* and the condition was that whatever the authorities said must be first *judged* by the individual based on his understanding of the Bible.

Private judgment was specifically included in the Reformed confessions of faith as one of the legitimate sources of knowledge, on the same level as church councils, and in need to be judged by the Word of God just as much as the opinions of the church councils:

> The supreme judge by which all controversies of religion are to be determined, and all decrees of councils, opinions of ancient writers, doctrines of men, and private spirits, are to be examined, and in whose sentence we are to rest, can be no other but the Holy Spirit speaking in the Scripture (WCF 1:10; LBCF 1:10).

On this basis, and on the basis of their struggles against the prelacy, the early Presbyterians in Scotland, as well as the Puritans and other dissenters in England, developed the concept of private judgment as an application of the priesthood of all believers to the position of a fundamental doctrine of the Reformed faith. Among a small modern sect today who claim to be spiritual heirs of the Scottish Covenanters, it is fashionable to lambast private judgment and to extol collective decisions of churchian "councils" as if they are the last time the Holy Spirit has spoken (similar to the

20. Martin Luther, "Right and Power of a Christian Church."

Romanists after the Council of Trent). The truth, however, is that the original Covenanters trusted private judgment far more than any modern theologians naming the Reformed traditions. No less an authority than George Gillespie witnesses against them:

> The subordinate judgment, which I call private, is the judgment of discretion whereby every Christian, for the certain information of his own mind, and the satisfaction of his own conscience, may and ought to try and examine, as well the decrees of councils as the doctrine of particular pastors, and in so far to receive and believe the same, as he understands them to agree with the Scriptures (*A Dispute Against The English Popish Ceremonies*).

Gillespie was consistent when it came to Presbyterianism. He actually denied the right even of a Presbyterian government to discard private judgment:

> The prelates did not allow men to examine, by the judgment of Christians and private discretion, their decrees and canons, so as to search the Scriptures and look at the warrants, but would needs have men think it enough to know the things to be commanded by them that are in places of power. Presbyterial government doth not lord it over men's consciences, but admitteth (yea commendeth) the searching of the Scriptures, whether these things that it holds forth be not so, and doth not press men's consciences with *sic volo, sic jubeo* [thus I will, thus I command], but desireth they may do in faith what they do (*Aaron's Rod Blossoming*, 1646).

Earlier in that same book, Gillespie contends that when a church is not doing its job as a church, individual Christians have the right to leave, have no obligation to obey the church, and that they even have the right to speak to it with the same spirit as the prophets, *quoting Calvin himself to this regard*:

> They, therefore, who give their will for a law, and their authority for a reason, and answer all the arguments of their opponents, by bearing down with the force of public constitution and the judgment of superiors, to which theirs must be conformed, do rule the Lord's flock "with force and with cruelty" (Ezek. 34:4); as "lords over God's heritage" (1 Pet. 5:3) Always, since men give us no leave to try their decrees and constitutions, that we may hold fast to no more than is good, God be thanked that we have a warrant to do it (without their leave) from his own word (1 Thess. 5:21) . . . "If we rightly feel we are deprived of the faculty of questioning, it must be indicated by that same spirit who speaks through his prophets," says Calvin. We will not then call any man rabbi nor, "*jurare in verba magistri*" [swear on the word of the master], nor yet be Pathagorean disciples to the church herself, but we will believe her and obey her in so far only as she is the pillar and ground of the truth (*A Dispute Against The English Popish Ceremonies*).

Apparently, the original Covenanters were much more Biblical than modern Presbyterians and Reformed Baptists, being willing to both listen to prophets outside the church and to speak to the church as prophets outside it, with the same Spirit who moved the prophets.

Francis Turretin went as far as to say that individuals guided by the Holy Spirit were more capable of finding out the meaning of Scripture:

> Rather we hold only that private believers gifted with the Holy Spirit are bound to examine according to the Word of God, whatever is proposed for their belief or practice by the rulers of the church; as much as by individuals separately as by many congregated in a synod. Also they are to believe that by the guidance of the Spirit, by pious prayers and diligent study of the Scriptures, they can better find out the meaning of Scripture in things necessary to salvation than whole synods receding from the Word of God and than a society which claims for itself (but falsely) the name of the true church (*Institutes of Elenctic Theology*, 1696).

According to Turretin, this duty is part of our "indispensable" office as priests and is meant to protect them against church tyranny and bondage:

> That cannot, therefore, be considered rashness or pride which belongs to the execution of an indispensable office imposed upon all believers. Nor under the pretext of avoiding pride ought believers to blind themselves and to divest themselves of their right in order that their consciences by a blind obedience may be reduced to bondage (*Ibid.)*.

Turretin concludes that individual Christians not only do not owe anyone any obedience in matters of conscience, but such obedience would actually put their souls in danger:

> But in affairs of conscience which have reference to faith, piety and the worship of God, no one can usurp dominion over the conscience; nor are we bound to obey anyone, because otherwise we would be bound to error and impiety and thus we would incur eternal punishment and our con-

> sciences would be stained with vices without criminality because we would be bound to obey superiors absolutely (*Ibid.*).

But these were Presbyterians. What about Reformed Baptists? The world has never had a more stout defender of private judgment against *all* human authority than the Prince of Preachers, Charles Spurgeon. Examples from his sermons are too many to list, so I will present only a representative sample. The clearest of all is in his sermon on Luke 12:54–57, where he identifies private judgment and resistance against authority with "manliness of spirit":

> He charges them to use their common sense, and not submit themselves to be hoodwinked by their leaders. He asked, "Judge you not even of yourselves what is right?" Why bow yourselves down that scribes and Pharisees may go over you? Think and judge for yourselves like men. The Lord, here, declares the duty of private judgment, and exhorts the people to use it, urging them to yield no more a slavish obedience to the mandates of their false leaders, but to use their own wits as they would upon ordinary matters, and even of themselves judge what was right. The people needed awakening from spiritual slumber. They required to be exhorted to manliness of spirit, for they had so completely surrendered their judgments to their blind leaders, that the most conspicuous signs of the time were unperceived by them.

Obviously then, the modern insistence of Christians submitting to the "care of pastors" would lead to "un-manliness" of spirit. One doesn't create true men by making them dependent on someone else's care and direction. Manliness is produced by maturity, and maturity is produced by the ability of a man to deal with challenges alone, with the invisible God, against all visible odds. The call for all to find a type of "safe space" under leaders will only create immature men, especiall when such leaders are neither proven legitimate nor mature themselves. We have too many of these immature men already. We need Spurgeon's manliness of spirit. For this we need private judgment to resist all human authority—yes, even that of "good" "solid" modern churches who act as if they have more authority than they really do.

The "right and duty of private judgment" was so dear a doctrine to Spurgeon that he was willing to break ties with his Baptist brethren over it as one of the most important doctrines of Protestantism. In 1888, he offered his resignation as a member of the Baptist Union of Great Britain and Ireland. His dissatisfaction with the Union was that it allowed membership to people who were questioning or rejecting basic Biblical doctrines. A delegation from the Union was promptly sent to Spurgeon. His reply to the delegation was that the Union needed to have a "simple basis of Bible truths. These are usually described as Evangelical doctrines." He then gave the delegation the following list (notice the order in which they were given):

1. The Divine inspiration, authority, and efficiency of the Holy Scriptures.
2. *The right and duty of private judgment in the interpretation of the Holy Scriptures.*
3. The Unity of the Godhead, and the Trinity of Persons therein.
4. The utter depravity of human nature in consequence of the fall.
5. The incarnation of the Son of God. His work of atonement for sinners of mankind, and His mediatorial intercession and reign.

6. The justification of the sinner by faith alone.
7. The work of the Holy Spirit in the conversion and sanctification of the sinner.
8. The immortality of the soul, the resurrection of the body, the judgment of the world by our Lord Jesus Christ, with the eternal blessedness of the righteous, and the eternal punishment of the wicked.
9. The Divine institution of the Christian ministry, and the obligation and perpetuity of the ordinances of Baptism and the Lord's Supper.[21]

These were the doctrinal priorities of the Prince of Preachers. The right to private judgment is in second place, after the importance of the Holy Scriptures, before everything else. He was a good Calvinist, after all, and like Calvin in his *Institutes*, started his priorities from the knowledge of God, which could only come from Scripture through private judgment in interpretation. The Divine institution of Christian ministry comes last. What about the Baptist confessional requirement for "local church membership"? It is nowhere on the list.

Returning to the Presbyterian camp, Charles Hodge also makes private judgment the mark of the Protestant faith, and relates it to the centrality and the perspicuity of Scripture. He dedicates a whole section to "Private Judgment" in his *Systematic Theology*. Here is what one of the greatest theologians in the history of Presbyterianism has to say on this issue:

> What Protestants deny on this subject is, that Christ has appointed any officer, or class of officers, in his Church to whose interpretation of the Scrip-

21. *The Baptist Quarterly Review*, Vol. X (London: Trübner and Co., 1888), p. 224.

> tures the people are bound to submit as of final authority. What they affirm is that He has made it obligatory upon every man to search the Scriptures for himself, and determine on his own discretion what they require him to believe and to do.[22]

Echoing Turretin's statement of the danger of obeying men on matters of faith and conscience, Hodge continues:

> Every man is responsible for his religious faith and his moral conduct. He cannot transfer that responsibility to others; nor can others assume it in his stead. He must answer for himself; and if he must answer for himself, he must judge for himself. It will not avail him in the day of judgment to say that his parents or his Church taught him wrong. He should have listened to God, and obeyed Him rather than men.[23]

We will talk later of the real meaning of church discipline, and how in the Bible, contrary to modern practices, it has absolutely nothing to do with church elders. Hodge makes the correct observation that divine admonishments in the Bible are always directed at the people in general, not at their elders. The people do not need anyone to stand between them and God in understanding Scripture:

> The Scriptures are everywhere addressed to the people, and not to the officers of the Church either exclusively, or specially. The prophets were sent to the people, and constantly said, "Hear, O Israel," "Hearken, O ye people." Thus, also, the discourses of Christ were addressed to the people, and the people heard him gladly. All the Epistles of the

22. Charles Hodge, *Systematic Theology*, Vol. 1, ch. 6, sec. 5.
23. *Ibid.*

> New Testament are addressed to the congregation, to the "called of Jesus Christ;" "to the beloved of God;" to those "called to be saints;" "to the sanctified in Christ Jesus;" "to all who call on the name of Jesus Christ our Lord;" "to the saints which are in (Ephesus), and to the faithful in Jesus Christ;" or "to the saints and faithful brethren which are in (Colosse);" and so in every instance. It is the people who are addressed. To them are directed these profound discussions of Christian doctrine, and these comprehensive expositions of Christian duty. They are everywhere assumed to be competent to understand what is written, and are everywhere required to believe and obey what thus came from the inspired messengers of Christ. They were not referred to any other authority from which they were to learn the true import of these inspired instructions. It is, therefore, not only to deprive the people of a divine right, to forbid the people to read and interpret the Scriptures for themselves; but it is also to interpose between them and God, and to prevent their hearing his voice, that they may listen to the words of men.[24]

This, of course, is in agreement with the description of the New Covenant in Hebrews 8:11 and Jeremiah 31:34. The quotes from Charles Hodge in this regard are also so numerous that we will have to limit them, but the last is important, for it not only defends the right to private judgment, it establishes our *duty* to resist any alleged church "minister" who wants to mandate submission to a human authority:

> It need hardly be remarked that this right of private judgment is the great safeguard of civil and religious liberty.

24. *Ibid.*

The principle of the right and duty of private judgment is not limited to Presbyterians and Baptists; it is common to all reformed Christians. Reformed Anglican Bishop J. C. Ryle, recently praised even by John MacArthur in a sermon as a Reformed authority, believed so strongly in private judgment that he wrote a separate paper on it: "Private Judgment."

Ryle describes what won the victory for the Protestant Reformation:

> There were three great doctrines or principles which won the battle of the Protestant Reformation. These three were:
>
> (1) the sufficiency and supremacy of Holy Scripture,
>
> (2) the right of private judgment, and
>
> (3) justification by faith only, without the deeds of the law.

The whole article is an amazing defense of the right, duty, and necessity of private judgment, but one line is particularly important to us here, for in it, Ryle comes to the logical conclusion of the concept of private judgment: that is, that *a true Christian has the right and the duty to stand alone against the whole Church* when necessary! Local churches all come and go, but a Christian must stand on the truth of God, even if that means to stand alone. Yes, this is an Anglican Bishop saying it:

> The *particular branches of the Church are not infallible.* Any one of them may err. Many of them have fallen foully, or have been swept away. Where is the Church of Ephesus at this day? Where is the Church of Sardis at the present time? Where is Augustine's Church of Hippo in Africa? Where is Cyprian's Church of Carthage? They are all gone!

> Not a vestige of any of them is left! *Shall we then be content to err — merely because the Church errs?* Will our company be any excuse for our error? Will our *erring in company* with the Church remove our responsibility for our own souls? Surely it is a thousand times better for a man to stand alone and be saved — than to err in company with the Church, and be lost! It is better to "prove all things" — and go to Heaven; than to say, "I dare not think for myself" — and go to Hell!

Today's tenacious Baptist proponents should pay attention: it should be particularly alarming to them that Presbyterians and even Episcopals have a superior view of Christian liberty and the rights and duties of the individual against the church. This is a very good sign that in ecclesiology, they are not really Reformed, but have rather gone over to the practice of Rome—or worse, pagans—making themselves little popes. Granted, they may only be listening to other Baptist preachers they respect and esteem, but this may very well turn out to be a dangerous trust. For many Baptist ministers in America today are nothing more than practical papists in their view of their own congregations.

To this list of Reformed theologians who held the right and duty of private judgment to be the distinguishing mark of the Reformation, we can add other theologians like Heinrich Bullinger, Philip Melanchthon, A. A. Hodge, John Owen, James Henley Thornwell, Robert Dabney, Richard Baxter, and many others. Obviously, the doctrine of private judgment was considered one of the most important doctrines of the Reformation and in the history of Reformed theology, no matter which part or group of the Reformed family one chooses. In fact, it is how the Reformation started: with Luther's firm affirmation of his right and duty to private judgment before a court of the political and church elite of the day:

> Unless I am convinced by the testimony of the Holy Scriptures or by evident reason—for I can believe neither pope nor councils alone, as it is clear that they have erred repeatedly and contradicted themselves—I consider myself convicted by the testimony of Holy Scripture, which is my basis; my conscience is captive to the Word of God. Thus I cannot and will not recant, because acting against one's conscience is neither safe nor sound. God help me. Amen.

It is for this reason the first thing Luther did after the Diet of Worms was not to establish a new church hierarchy, but *to translate the Bible into the language of the people, so that the people could exercise their right and duty of private judgment.*

To make it simple: without the right and duty of private judgment, there is no Reformation, and we are back to Papism.

Is it not strange, then, that the modern self-professing Reformed celebrities never even mention this doctrine, and very few, if any, of modern Reformed Christians have ever even heard of the doctrine and its importance for the Reformation? John MacArthur has had 30-plus years of preachings, and a search on his name and "private judgment" yields no results. Same applies to Albert Mohler. Same applies to John Piper. Same applies to Michael Horton. Same applies to R. Scott Clark, and all the other names at Westminster West. Same applies to R. C. Sproul. Same applies to a number of other modern Reformed celebrities. I do not follow Apologia Radio and I can't find any database of its topics, but when I asked people who follow it, they can't remember him ever speaking on the issue of private judgment. I have never heard a sermon on private judgment in any "Reformed" church I have been to. None of my Reformed friends can remember such a sermon or lecture ever, neither in church or at any seminary. I have some people who have been Presbyterians their whole lives and have been through hundreds and thousands of sermons and lectures, but when I mention "private judgment," they are all against it. All are deeply surprised when I tell them that it was one of the most important doctrines of the Reformation.

Any conscientious reader should be deeply alarmed by now. How is it that a doctrine that just 100 years ago was considered one of the cornerstones of the Reformation and of Protestantism is today so well-forgotten and never mentioned? What kind of "Reformed theology" have we been taught all this time? With so many claims of "Calvinist" revival in the churches today, how is it that the very doctrine that started the Reformation is missing?

The reason should be obvious: The doctrine of the right and duty of private judgment cannot coexist with the modern mythologies of mandatory "local church membership" and "submission to the local church."

Since according the Confessions, "The purest Churches under heaven are subject both to mixture and error; and some have so degenerated, as to become no Churches of Christ, but synagogues of Satan,"[25] the burden is laid on the individual believer, filled with the Holy Spirit, to judge every word and every teaching and every practice of any local church, and any pastor or elder or bishop. It is not just a *right* that he can exercise whenever he decides. It is a *duty* that he *must* exercise always, or, according to Turretin, "an indispensable office imposed upon all believers." Even more than that: the individual believer *must* exercise that office even when he is alone against the whole church, and the whole church is clearly in error, just as Paul did in Antioch (Gal. 2). Without this duty of the individual believer, there is no Reformation.

When the individual believer, however, is bound by a special covenant into "membership" and "submission" to a

25. WCF 25:5; LBCF 26:3.

local body—even if it is among the "purest churches under heaven"—this right and duty of private judgment is compromised. Granted, modern ecclesiocrats will be quick to admit that such submission is not absolute. What they do not say, however, is that under the terms "local church membership" their power to declare "excommunication" continues to be absolute, and their immunity to sanctions is also nearly absolute. That is, the individual believer is not absolutely bound to obey what the "elders" say, but the "elders" are still free to do whatever they want with him. (The situation is very similar to taxation: Paying taxes is legally called "voluntary," but the government will still put you in prison and confiscate your belongings if you do not pay.) The only challenge to their power will come when more and more people take seriously their right and duty of private judgment—for this is the same challenge that shook Rome in the Protestant Reformation.

When the individual believers have the right and duty of private judgment, then the whole concept of "submission to the local church" becomes meaningless. Submission is owed only when the local church is faithful to the Word of God. There is, however, no necessity for a special oath of "membership" for that, for such an oath has already been made in baptism. At the same time, when the local church opposes the Word of God, then what is owed is not submission but resistance and rebellion against the ungodly power of the "elders," not to mention sanctions against the session up to excommunication. Of course, no church session would include such a clause in their church's constitution today. That needs to be changed.

So the only solution for modern ecclesiocrats is to conveniently forget about the distinguishing mark of the Protestant Reformation—the doctrine of the right and duty of private judgment—and never mention it to their flocks. Though, to be fair, some of them may not be conveniently forgetting—they may never have ever been taught of it themselves. Whatever the cause, they instead return to a Papist and cultist ecclesiology which elevates the elite and frees it from any sanctions, while subjecting the individuals in the church to its power. In Rushdoony's words,

> [W]here a strong doctrine of the Spirit is not operative and governing, a strong doctrine of the church replaces it, so that institutional controls and government replace the Spirit.[26]

Conversely, in order to replace the Spirit with institutional controls, churchian elites need to rule out of the church the means by which the Spirit has always operated in opposition to them: private judgment through the individual consciences of men.

Thus, when John MacArthur complains about people moving from church to church, "never submitting to the care of elders," he accuses these people of "misunderstanding of the believer's responsibility to the body of Christ." The truth is, MacArthur only shows his neglect of the Biblical teaching and of Reformed theology. Under the principle of the right and duty of private judgment, *this is exactly what people should be doing: listening to sermons in the churches and judging the preachers according to the Word of God.* What MacArthur is really criticizing, and from which he apparently wants to be free, is accountability to the Holy Spirit acting through the private judgment of the individual believers. In the same way, when Jeff Durbin acts to silence the "facebook prophets," he is not speaking for God, and he is certainly not speaking as a Reformed minister. In typical Baptist tradition, though perhaps unwitingly, he really is attempting to free himself from accountability before the court of private judgment, which court was the most distinguished characteristic of the Protestant Reformation. Such an authoritarian statement coming from a stated church of-

26. R. J. Rushdoony, *Systematic Theology*, Vol. I, p. 296.

ficer cannot be speaking for the Church, and cannot claim to be speaking for the Holy Spirit. It was speaking for the interests of a corrupt church hierarchy, which, to borrow from Tertullian, "put to flight the Paraclete."[27]

27. *Against Praxeas*, ch. 1.

11. The Nature and Structure of the New Testament Church

By now, we have exposed a number of mythologies dear to modern churchmen. Mandatory "local church membership" and its related "vows" and "covenants" are novelties that arose from dictatorial cults and political pressure on the churches. They contribute nothing to accountability and church discipline; they have instead destroyed accountability and church discipline. "Submission" to the local church is not Biblical, either. It is another mythology designed to rob the faithful of their right and duty of private judgment—a right and duty for which many past saints have died.

For anyone who has been influenced by these mythologies, the question now remains: *What about church discipline and excommunication?* How are we supposed to do church then? How do we gather, as commanded in the New Testament? How do we practice church discipline, and especially excommunication, if there is no mandatory "local church membership"?

These are good questions, but they are not only easy to answer from a Biblical perspective, they are actually *not* answerable within the current paradigm of the church, contrary to all expectation and claims today. This is true precisely because the current paradigm was specifically designed to protect the ruling elites in the churches. Again, this is not a comprehensive treatise, but we can lay out some basic principles to understand how the church should be organized and where our efforts should be directed.[28]

28. For more comprehensive studies in the Biblical nature of the

Any study of the nature of the New Testament Church must start with the nature and the promise of the New Covenant. Obviously, if our idea of "church" doesn't serve the New Covenant declared in the Bible, then our idea of "church" is fallacious and will lead to disastrous results. The last century, at least, comes to mind.

One of the most important promises of the New Covenant was given in Jeremiah 31:33–34:

> "But this is the covenant which I will make with the house of Israel after those days," declares the LORD, "I will put My law within them and on their heart I will write it; and I will be their God, and they shall be My people. "They will not teach again, each man his neighbor and each man his brother, saying, 'Know the LORD,' for they will all know Me, from the least of them to the greatest of them," declares the LORD, "for I will forgive their iniquity, and their sin I will remember no more."

These verses are repeated in Hebrews 8:8–12, in the context of the difference between the Old and the New Covenant. The concept of the New Covenant as a Covenant in which every individual is directly taught by God—and therefore does not need human teachers—is repeated in Isa. 11:9; 54:13; John 6:45; Gal. 3:1; Phil. 3:15; 1 Thess. 4:9; and 1 John 2:20, 27. The very fact of giving the Holy Spirit to all who believe (the priesthood of all believers) should lead us to the conclusion that the New Covenant of God changes the standards for the religious hierarchy in the covenanted community. That hierarchy will have to abide by different

church as opposed to the modern concept of the church, see R. J. Rushdoony, *Institutes of Biblical Law*, Ch. 14; Stephen Perks, *The Nature, Government, and Function of the Church: A Reassessment*; *The Christian Passover: Agape Feast or Ritual Abuse*; and *The Problem of the Gifted Speaker*. All of Stephen Perks's books are available at The Kuyper Foundation, http://www.kuyper.org/.

rules than the Old Covenant hierarchy (Heb. 8:6), its function will be different than the function of the Old Covenant hierarchy, and its goal and purpose will be different than the goal and purpose of the old priesthood. The difference, obviously, is in *the nature of revelation*. This is the very presupposition at the very beginning of Hebrews, *that the nature of revelation has changed*:

> God, after He spoke long ago to the fathers in the prophets in many portions and in many ways, in these last days has spoken to us in His Son, whom He appointed heir of all things, through whom also He made the world (Heb. 1:1–2).

In this new covenantal context of revelation, clearly, the old systems of priestly-proxy—revelation by proxy, knowledge by proxy, growth by proxy, maturity by proxy—are all abolished. Men don't need to go to a special place and to a special class to learn about God and to grow in knowledge of the Lord. Christ has been revealed clearly to all, including to the "foolish Galatians." The right and duty of private judgment was based on two ideas: the Scriptures are plain to *all* who read them, and the Holy Spirit is given to *all* who believe. Men do not need to place themselves "under care" as immature children as a long-term goal of Christian life. The desired state for men is to be mature, trained to judge between good and evil, and ready to train others. They should become mature and trained enough *not* to need teachers and trainers.

Making this Biblical principle the foundation of our understanding of the role and function of the church should produce in us a radical change in the way we view the institutional church. In our churches today, as exhibited in the charge against "Facebook prophets," the institutional church is viewed as the purpose and end of the Christian life. It is viewed as "magisterial"—that is, as a ruler over the life of its individual members. Thus, the requirement for "submission." Any institution that views itself like this will assume the role of the proper guardian of all those under its magisterial rule—whether the institution itself is even *capable* of being a guardian or not. The call for Christians to gather in churches "under the care of elders" is no different than the call of the bramble for the trees to take refuge in its shade (Jotham's parable—Judges 9:7–15). This means that trees who have a history of productive life and maturity submit "under the care" of "elders" who seldom have anything more to show than their ability to get a seminary degree, jump through bureaucratic hoops, and get picked to be on church sessions. Once the church is accepted as the ruler over men's lives in this way, the maturity of the individual Christian becomes irrelevant to it. His gifts, calling, and productivity for the Kingdom of God likewise become irrelevant except to the extent they can serve the goals and agenda of the ruling elites. Otherwise they are missed, neglected, ignored, forgotten, surpressed, or even warned against. All that is relevant, therefore, is whether he serves his new master, the institutional church—even if that master never does anything of any value for the Kingdom of God, but is only concerned with its own bureaucratic, ceremonial existence.

The true Church of God, however, focused on the nature of the New Covenant, on the Holy Spirit abiding in every individual believer, and on the Kingdom of God, *is not concerned with gathering Christians under its shade, but just the opposite: scattering them throughout the world.* In the cosmic battle between the Church and the powers of evil, we are not the ones who have walls and gates. We are the ones who are flooding the world and besieging the walls and the gates of the enemy. Our job is not to build small churchdoms; it is to build the Kingdom. Only where there are people still untrained to build and fight must the institutional church be to offer training and healing; but for the mature who do not need training or healing, the institutional church cannot and should not be a drain on their energy and resources. They should be left alone to continue their fighting and building, in the world, in the civilization around the church.

Rushdoony saw the problem and wrote extensively on it in chapter 14 of his *Institutes*:

> The training of such mature men is the function of the church. The purpose of the church should not be to bring men into subjection to the church, but rather to train them into a royal priesthood capable of bringing the world into subjection to Christ the King. The church is the recruiting station, the training field, and the armory for Christ's army of royal priests. *It is a functional, not a terminal, institution.*
>
> The church has by and large paid lip service to the priesthood of all believers, because its hierarchy has distrusted the implications of the doctrine, and because it has seen the church as an end in itself, not as an instrument.[29]

This is exactly what is occuring in the criticism of "facebook prophets": it is not asking whether these men are mature and Biblical. It automatically accuses them for not being in subjection to an institutional church. But do they need such "subjection"? Does the institutional church offer any training or armory to be worth the subjection? Modern Baptist ecclesiocracy does not ask these questions. For it, the institutional church is an end in itself, not a means to training. Rushdoony continued by explaining the meaning of priesthood and the war of the church against it:

> The purpose of man's calling as priest is thus to realize himself as God's vicegerent and to dedicate himself, his areas of dominion, and his calling to

29. R.J. Rushdoony, *Institutes of Biblical Law*, Vol. I, p. 764.

> God and to the service of God's kingdom. Man's *self-realization* is possible only when man fulfills his priestly calling.
>
> The tendency of institutions—church, state, and school—and of callings, is to absolutize themselves and to play god in the lives of men. . . .[30]

In the Bible, some have noted an apparent contradiction between Jer. 31:34, where the New Covenant is described as all the people not needing teachers, and New Testament verses like Ephesians 4:11, where Paul legitimizes ministries of some authority, like apostles, prophets, evangelists, pastors, and teachers. Which is it, now? Is everyone knowledgeable enough so as not to need teachers? Or do we need teachers? The answer is in the view of the institutional church presented here: All the ministries of Ephesians 4 are given as a temporary measure for the growth of the body and of the individual believers, not for a permanent subjection of all believers at all times under an institution. The context of Ephesians 4 confirms the temporary character and need for such ministries, for it immediately adds the clause, "until":

> He gave some *as* apostles, and some *as* prophets, and some *as* evangelists, and some *as* pastors and teachers, for the equipping of the saints for the work of service, to the building up of the body of Christ; *until* we all attain to the unity of the faith, and of the knowledge of the Son of God, to a mature man, to the measure of the stature which belongs to the fullness of Christ (Eph. 4:11–13, emphasis added).

Very clearly, then, individual believers are not here for the institutional church, to serve the institutional church; that would be a gross perversion of the role of the individual

30. *Ibid.*, p. 765.

believers and of the institutional church. The Biblical view is that the institutional church must be there to serve the individual believers, and if it does not have the capacity to serve, no one needs it, and we had better not have it. Let's recall what we quoted earlier from the *First Book of Discipline* of the Kirk of Scotland (1560), that it is better not to have a church at all than to have a church of incapable ministers:

> We are not ignorant that the rarity of godly and learned men shall seem to some a just reason why that so strait and sharp examination should not be taken universally; for so it shall appear that the most part of kirks shall have no minister at all. But let these men understand that the lack of able men shall not excuse us before God if, by our consent, unable men be placed over the flock of Christ Jesus; as also that, amongst the Gentiles, godly, learned men were also rare as they are now amongst us, when the apostle gave the same rule to try and examine ministers which we now follow. And last, let them understand that it is alike to have no minister at all, and to have an idol in the place of a true minister; yea and in some cases, it is worse. For those that are utterly destitute of ministers will be diligent to search for them; but those that have a vain shadow do commonly, without further care, content themselves with the same, and so they remain continually deceived, thinking that they have a minister, when in very deed they have none.

Institutional church leadership, thus, is only legitimate when it serves that purpose. When it does not serve that purpose, it is illegitimate and deserves no honor whatsoever, no submission whatsoever, but only criticism and judgment through prophetic word, from prophets outside or inside the institutional church. The "membership" of the prophet does not have any covenantal significance; what matters is whether the word he speaks agrees with the Word of God and whether the leaders deserve the criticism. Thus, any churchman whose first concern is institutional "membership" and not the content of the message, is by default illegitimate and should not be rendered any honor.

Moreover—and this will come as a shocking surprise for many modern Christians in America—church leadership is not necessary for the being and the operation of the Church. Yes, you read that well: *church leadership is not necessary for the being and the operation of the Church.* It is only necessary for the *well*-being of the Church, and that only in specific circumstances, where needed. We already saw this concept above in a quotation from the First London Baptist Confession (1644), that local churches are not defined by having leadership, but have the power, *for their well-being,* to choose elders. The churches, apparently, are legitimate churches even *before* they have elders, and thus without elders—a concept which the Second London Confession missed, thus creating an unresolvable conundrum. At least one modern Presbyterian denomination has adopted thisconcept of the leadership being functional but not necessary:

> The presbyterian form of government seeks to fulfill these scriptural requirements for the glory of Christ, the edification of the church, and the enlargement of that spiritual liberty in which Christ has set us free. *Nevertheless, while such scriptural government is necessary for the perfection of church order, it is not essential to the existence of the church visible* (*Book of Church Order* of the Orthodox Presbyterian Church, I.3, emphasis added).

The early church, as described in Acts, operated without the ecclesiastical office of elders most of the time. In many situations, Paul would create many disciples in a place and would not "plant a church" with "elders" (see, for example, Acts 14:21). The same principle could be seen in Acts 14:23: elders were appointed to every church in the area, but only on the way back to Antioch. For some time at least, the churches there existed without elders. Paul must have found it necessary for the specific situation and circumstances in the churches in Phrygia and Lycaonia (parts of Galatia) to appoint elders. One reason could be that, unlike other churches, these were almost entirely composed of converted Gentiles, and therefore there was no previous foundation in the Law of God in the churches. (Perhaps that's why these churches were so easily misled by itinerant Jewish preachers, which is the topic of Galatians.) To compare, the Epistle to the Hebrews—who should have known the Law—expects the Hebrews to be mature and independent and chastises them for needing teachers (Heb. 5:11–14).

A *requirement* that churches have elders, therefore, cannot be seen anywhere in the New Testament. Sure, elders are mentioned, and the requirements for an elder are mentioned, but that is different from a mandatory establishment of elders or local church hierarchy. In all his epistles, Paul speaks to whole congregations without mentioning elders, even where he speaks on issues of church discipline, as in his two epistles to the Corinthians. He sent Titus to Crete to appoint elders, but even in this action, two things are obvious: *first*, Crete had legitimate churches without elders before the arrival of Titus. *Second*, there was a very special reason for the necessity of ordaining elders: the immorality of the Cretans and the divisions in their churches (Titus 1:10–16). Logically, even the very criteria for elders that Paul gives to Titus already show that Titus might not be able to ordain elders in every city: There was no guarantee that every city would have at least one believer who fit the description in Titus 1:6–9.

The modern concept that the universal Church should grow more and more visible in its power and jurisdiction is therefore nonsensical in the light of the Biblical message. The growth of the institutional church in power and influence—as an institution—will be a testimony not to the success but to the *failure* of the New Covenant. The promise in the Bible is not that the institutional church will grow, but that the Kingdom and the knowledge of God will grow until there is no need for teachers, and therefore no need for an institutional church. The more the institutional church insists on growth and power, the more it declares that it expects its members to remain immature and incompetent. That is where the American church is today, after over 100 years of dominance of the concept of mandatory "local church membership": millions of sermons, lectures, conferences, Bible camps, crusades, etc., have produced nothing of value, and the church continues losing the cultural war. Why? In large part, because the churches do not see themselves as servants for the maturity of the people, but as rulers over flocks that are expected to remain immature throughout their lives. "Under the care of elders" sounds like something very pious and righteous; the reality is, it is the killer of maturity.

The visible Church, then, as defined by the Reformed Confessional standards, must be understood to consist of "all those throughout the world that profess the true religion; and of their children."[31] "All those" are all individuals, for the requirement is profession of faith. Some may decide to organize themselves in societies with formal membership; others may decide to stay out of all kinds of secondary commitments and retain only membership in the universal Church through baptism. Membership in such societies cannot be considered an automatic proof of membership in the universal church, and non-membership can not be considered an automatic exclusion from the Church. Some may decide to keep more informal connections to other Christians, others may decide to work alone in areas where there

31. WCF 25:2.

is a need to work alone. While regularly gathering together is important, it is not such a pressing necessity as to be a priority over certain occupations for the Kingdom of Christ which may require certain levels of solitude.

We have a number of faithful Christians in the history of the church who withdrew from commitments to church collectives and still remained faithful to the universal Church and rendered an immense service to the body of Christ. In our most recent history, one such example is A. W. Pink, whose story is probably one of the most radical stories of "lone rangers" ever told. For the last 16 years of his life he never joined any church, nor even a local informal fellowship, and devoted all his time to writing his books. Yet today, no Baptist ever complains of this deliberate choice to remain alone, and there is hardly a Reformed Baptist home in the U.S. today that does not have at least one book by Pink. Examples like Pink are more numerous than most people realize, but what is more important is that Pink's real ministry of writing books was frustrated and almost ruined by his earlier attempts to fit into a local community. The mandatory commitment of such men to a local congregation, investing effort and time in it, whether it may exist some time down the road or not, is a gigantic waste of spiritual resource. The "democratic" impulse in modern churches—especially in Baptist churches—to test men of strategic calling and ministry by sending them to sweep floors, teach day care, and change diapers in the nursery makes no sense whatsoever. While it is commendable that all men learn to change diapers (we have changed many), such a religion of works does not prove anything about the character of a man and really does not teach him anything beyond the basics, which, for would-be ministers, should have been leared long ago. All this mentality does is deprive the church of valuable time which could have been used in writing, teaching, training, evangelizing, or anything else.

Local communities and gatherings, of course, will always

exist (*probably*, as Charles Hodge said). Some of them will require some sort of a covenant or oath to join: mainly because such organizations will have to deal with questions of church property and monetary decisions, or public declarations of faith, vision, and mission, and such collective decisions must be limited to sworn members who have made a commitment with all rights and responsibilities to the local group. Such organizations, however, are no more representative of the Church universal than any individual who believes in Christ and practices his faith in the world around him. Neither do they have the moral right to exclude from the Church and from fellowship other groups or individuals who profess the same faith but do not have the same structure or the same form of collective commitment or oath. Local congregations may have a system of leadership, or may not—local church government is not necessary for the existence of the church, only for its *well*-being.

More importantly, membership in such groups or congregations must not be based on any requirement to "join a church." Every believer has joined the Church at the moment of his baptism. Nothing more is required of him in terms of oaths or membership. In the words of A. A. Hodge, "A church has no right to make a condition of membership anything that Christ has not made a condition of salvation."[32] Any baptized person who professes the faith and practices it is a legitimate member of any congregation anywhere. If a congregation excludes Christians from fellowship and communion only on the basis that they have not taken a particular oath of commitment to a particular local group, such congregation declares itself to be schismatic in relation to the Church Universal. Such congregation does not confess together with the rest of the Church that "we believe One Holy Catholic and Aposolic Church."

The foundation for unity must be the Word of God, not

32. A. A. Hodge, *A Commentary on the Confession of Faith* (Philadelphia: Presbyterian Board of Education, 1869), 21.

local visible organizations. The goal and purpose must be the growth of the Kingdom of God, Christendom—a Christian civilization which expands way beyond any local church or club or family. Local congregations, if they want more people to join them, must do it through offering superior services of training people to expand the Kingdom. If a local congregation cannot offer such services, it is useless. It is better if it dissolves; as many local congregations have dissolved throughout history without any visible damage to the growing Kingdom of God. The local congregation cannot be an end in itself; it cannot be a ruler to whom we must submit. It is not and can not be magisterial. A local congregation must be *ministerial*: a servant who serves Christians to achieve purposes greater than itself. If it is useless as a servant, it must be dismissed. If it exists only for the purposes of ceremonial repetition every Sunday, its members should leave it. It is better not to have a local congregation than to be a member of a useless one. Where it serves well and has elders who lead and teach well, it deserves double honor (1 Tim. 5:17). Even then, formal membership must be voluntary and conditional. For an individual, membership in an organization is subject to a number of reasonable limitations, from his personal gifts and calling to the spiritual health and strategic importance of the organization itself.

In other words, "local church membership," for all it is worth, must be left to Christian liberty. Any preacher or teacher who demands such membership as the condition for membership in the universal Church, is preaching another Gospel, and, in the words of Charles Hodge, "introduces a new method of salvation."

12. The Biblical Way of Church Discipline

The last objection we need to take care of is this: "What do we do with church discipline if we do not have mandatory local church membership?" In the mind of many modern churchgoers, the only way to do church discipline is through the "local church" and through "membership in the local church." So, how would we do it when such "membership" is not mandatory?

We already saw above that historically, there is absolutely no reason to believe that "local church membership" ever helps with church discipline. To the contrary, we have ample evidence that the rise of this doctrine led only to the decline of discipline in the churches. There is a good reason for this: *the very idea that church discipline can be maintained through local churches actually makes no sense whatsoever.* It is not that we have not applied "local church membership" correctly, and thus do not have good results. It is that the very concept *leads* to undesired results. It is just like government schools: it is not that they have failed; they have succeeded in what they were meant to do. In the same way, it is not that "local church membership" has failed in its task of maintaining discipline. To the contrary, it has succeeded in its task to destroy it.

What in the world am I talking about? How could one arrive at such extreme conclusions? Three specific and direct examples from my personal experience with "local church discipline" in America will help us see the utter absurdity of the concept.

1. The Abandonment of Luke 12:48.

About ten years ago, a friend of mine invited me to visit his church—a church of good reputation, part of a large Presbyterian denomination—one Sunday morning and "participate in the fellowship." My displeasure with the "service" must have been written all over my face, so after we got out of the church, he asked me to give him my "brutally honest opinion" about the "service." We had the following dialogue:

I started: "Well, since you want my brutally honest opinion, this preacher you have there is not qualified to be a preacher or even an elder. His sermon—or whatever passed for a sermon—was full of nonsensical clichés and repetitions. It had nothing whatsoever in it that would be beneficial to even a newly converted Christian. My ten-year-old daughter can make up a better sermon. The man can't teach, and having him as an elder violates the clear command of 1 Timothy 3:2 and Titus 1:9."

"Yeah, you are right, and we all know that. It's just the ruling elders have not been able to find a better teacher yet, and this one has his seminary degrees. But you know, people don't come to church for the sermon."

"Yeah? What do they come to church for?"

"For the fellowship."

"For the fellowship? I didn't see much fellowship in there. Everyone was sitting quietly and staring at the guys on the podium. You and I can have more fellowship over a glass of bourbon tonight than you can have at 50 of those services."

"I meant fellowship after church. The potluck and the rest of it."

"Oh, if everyone comes not for the sermon but for the fellowship, can you be a member and only come for the potluck after church?"

"No, I have to come for the service."

"What will happen if you only come for the fellowship?"

"They will probably excommunicate me."

"Let me see if I get this right. You have elders who can't meet their specific Biblical requirement to be able to teach, and you are willing to excuse them from this requirement and obligation, but you have already given them the power to excommunicate you, which is nowhere specifically granted to elders?"

"Huh, I see what you are saying."

His is not the only church with this problem. I cannot count how many times I have heard the phrase, "People don't go to church for the sermon," as an excuse for the lack of qualifications of their elders. Even more often I have heard the more general excuse: "You shouldn't be looking for a perfect church and perfect elders." Of course. But then, these less than perfect elders want for themselves the power to declare discipline, and even excommunicate, as if they are perfect. That is, we give power to people who, by their own admission, are not qualified to wield it, and we don't even see the problem in it.

This is a clear violation of the principle in Luke 12:48: "From everyone who has been given much, much will be required." Those who are given the power of discipline and excommunication should be held to a stricter standard, and should be always as near as possible to the ideal set forth in 1 Timothy 3:1–7 and Titus 1:5–8. When Paul gave these instructions for elders, he did not tell Timothy and Titus, "but if you cannot find such people, just appoint somebody; we are not looking for perfect elders anyway." To excuse the elders of a church from being held up to these standards, because "we can't have perfect elders," and at the same time giving them the ultimate power of excommunication is a clear violation of the principles in Scripture concerning power and discipline.

2. The Abandonment of Deut. 19:18–19 and of Luke 7:8

In the second example from my experience with "church discipline" in the modern "local churches," I was present at an appeal trial before a presbytery as a higher adjudicatory. The case was the unlawful excommunication of a local church member by his session for alleged "disrespect to authority." The presbytery found the decisions of the session inconsistent with justice, as well as motivated by personal feelings, and promptly reversed the verdict and restored the man to full membership in his church. It seemed like most of the people in the room were happy with the decision—with the exception of some of the elders in question, of course.

I had the chance afterward to fellowship with two of the judges on the trial, and I used the chance to ask them a question: "So what happens to that session now? Will the Presbytery excommunicate them as a session?"

It turned out they never even considered such an option. But as we continued talking, the two men came to realize that in order for them to be consistent, this would be the only logical thing for them to do. The session had committed injustice. They had testified falsely against the man, and they had judged falsely against him. The session as a collective of power had conspired against an innocent man, using its legal power to inflict on him a punishment he did not deserve. Under the principle of Deut. 19:18–19, there could be no neutral reversal of the verdict. Any reversal of that verdict should be by default a verdict on the false accusers, with the same punishment inflicted on them. These men should have been automatically excommunicated from their church and from the denomination, and not allowed to return until there was public repentance. Of all things, they certainly should not have been allowed to remain in leadership positions in the church, on any excuse whatsoever. One such grave injustice should disqualify them forever.

Yet, even as they agreed with me on the ethics of punishing the false accusers with the same punishment they planned for their victim, the two men were reluctant to pursue their actions to their logical Biblical end. The reason? It was not part of their Book of Discipline. It could not be included either, for under the current ecclesiology, there was no way to include a principle which would subject the sessions to the same sanctions they can mete out to their church members. Which means, the principle of the centurion in Luke 7:8, "a man under authority, with men under his authority," which Jesus praised so highly as "such faith I have not found even in Israel," also has been abandoned in our churches.

3. The Abandonment of Matt. 18:15–20.

In my third example, I was present at a conversation between pastors of two churches. In that conversation, an issue was brought up about a man excommunicated from one of those two churches, who just went down the road and became a "member" of the other. To my amazement, the conversation was quite friendly and rather nonchalant about the whole matter. It was as if I was listening to two employers who just exchanged an employee between them. One just did not want the guy, the other was fine to have him. It was as if the excommunication never happened, as if there were no charges against the excommunicated person, as if all excommunication involved was sending a person to another "local church."

After the meeting, I asked the pastor of the "excommunicating" church, "You don't seem to be taking your own verdict very seriously. I thought you would be consistent with it and either try to convince or excommunicate the other church for taking in a person whom you have delivered to Satan, according to Paul's words in 1 Timothy 1:20." The pastor simply shrugged, "Nothing can be done about it. All I can do is rid my church of that man."

He explained to me that he had been very meticulous in his application of Matthew 18:15–20. However, when I read the verses to him and asked him if he believed that the verdict of his church was also the verdict of God, he was not so sure about it. Maybe, maybe not. Apparently, he also believed in some sort of neutral stance in God, for in his view, even if his verdict was not the verdict of God—that is, even if his church had committed injustice—God would not see it as a big issue. Either way, there was no use in trying to convince the church universal in the validity of his church's verdict. "Tell it to the church" meant nothing to him beyond "tell it to our local church." In other words, *church discipline for him was simply banning the person from a particular local group*, nothing more.

These three examples are not isolated. In the context of our modern churches, "discipline"—no matter how much modern ecclesiocrats beat their chests over that term—means nothing whatsoever. It has become a joke. No one views it seriously, not even the ecclesiocrats themselves. The majority of Christians laugh at their fake discipline, and the ecclesiocrats laugh at it, too—in private, of course. Any "excommunicated" person just switches "churches," and can pretty much forget about his old "church." Given the rate of change and the longevity of "local churches" these days, he can be pretty sure his old "church" will barely exist a few years down the road, and even if it does, it will hardly be the same. Or, if it remains the same, it will hardly be relevant to anything outside it. Inside the churches themselves, "discipline" is simply a tool of control. It is seldom a tool for doctrinal or ethical purity. Any "discipline" is only "discipline" for the ordinary members of the churches. Those who have achieved some "leadership" status are hardly affected by it, except in some very egregious cases. It certainly never applies to "leaders" in packs, also known as "church sessions" or "presbyteries," where any injustice or immorality may meet a mild reproach—if that much at all—and a maximum verdict of "reversal of decision."

Some will say, that such cases are merely a few bad apples but not the whole church. But this is not true. If anything, there are a few good apples in a basket full of rottenness, and it is just a matter of time until they become rotten as well.

Others will argue that the system is good, it is just that we have not applied it well. This is not true either. It is similar to the old claim that "Communism is a great idea, it was just applied by bad people."

The truth is, the current state of the church is not an accident: it follows directly from the currently dominant ecclesiology in the churches, that of mandatory "local church membership." It is because of mandatory "local church membership" that we have "elders" who do not and cannot meet the requirements for elders. It is because of mandatory "local church membership" that we have church sessions who cannot be held responsible for the injustices they commit. It is because of mandatory "local church membership" that excommunication has become a joke, and nobody really pays attention to it. The self-ghettoization of the Church into little, self-absorbed, fragmented "communities" that seek to suck the energy and time of their members for trivial tasks and purposes of no lasting significance has led to the situation today. Discipline is not created nor maintained by fragmented ghettos; the whole concept that "local churches" and their "elders" can maintain church discipline is not only seriously flawed, it is outright absurd.

So how is church discipline maintained, then, in a Biblical fashion, without mandatory "local church membership"? Here is how:

Church Discipline Is Learning, Not Punishments

The obsession with ecclesiastical punishments—and especially with excommunication—is not Biblical. While excommunication is mentioned in the Bible, it does not constitute such a great part of the life of the church as it is assumed today. We have only three passages dealing with excommunication: Matthew 18:15–20; 1 Corinthians 5:9–13; and 2 Thessalonians 3:6–13. The three passages are certainly not exhaustive in detail. To make them the foundation of the modern doctrine of excommunication as "church discipline" means that we would need to impose on the text some preconceived ideas. When we get to the modern detailed books of church courts and discipline—full of details that cannot be found anywhere in the Bible—the deviation of the modern churches from the Biblical teaching is clear.

The reason for such deviation is that the modern churches have adopted an essentially pagan view of discipline: *that discipline is the same as punishment.* It is under the secularist "natural law" worldview that a man is considered "disciplined" when he is mindful of the punishments his superiors may impose on him. Paganism has no trust in the self-government of individuals, so individuals are always kept in line through being constantly threatened when they go exploring outside the limits set by the dominant institutional hierarchy. Thus, in paganism, there can be no discipline without institutional control; a person is either under the power ("under the care") of institutional superiors, or he is labeled an "anarchistic" or a "rebel" and called "undisciplined." That a person can be disciplined simply based on his self-control under God is an unacceptable notion in any paganism.

Modern churches, having accepted this pagan idea of "discipline," boast of having "discipline" when they have a system of inquisiting and punishing them. Take any Book of Church Order and read the chapters on discipline. They always have to do with court procedures and punishments. Outside court procedures and punishments, outside institutional power and control, there is no discipline. Thus, only people who are under such control—"members"—are "disciplined." Procedure and punishments constitute the vast bulk, if not the whole, of discipline in these systems.

R. J. Rushdoony noted this pagan nature of the modern notion of discipline and called it "not discipline at all." He pointed to the problem directly:

> Failure to understand this distinction between discipline and punishment is responsible for much of

> the disorder in the church. In almost every church, where *discipline* is spoken of, in reality *punishment* is meant. In the confusion of the two, it is discipline that is usually lost.[33]

He then gives the correct, Biblical meaning of "discipline":

> [D]iscipline comes from disciple, which is the Latin word *discipulus*, in turn derived from *disco*, learn. *To be a disciple and to be under discipline is to be a learner in a learning process. If there is no learning, and no growth in learning, there is no discipline.*[34]

He continues by pointing out that "an undisciplined church is a church where there is a failure in the proclamation and teaching of Scripture." Thus, "membership" in such a church does not lead to discipline; it is destructive to true Biblical discipline. There is more true discipline in a lone man with his Bible and the Holy Spirit than in a church where the Word of God is not preached, or is only preached at a very rudimentary, fundamental level, keeping the hearers ona diet of milk (Heb. 6:1–2) and constantly immature.

Such, however, are the vast majority of churches in the U.S. today. While the author of Hebrews clearly says (5:11–6:2) that we should strive to maturity and not remain on the level of the basic doctrines of the faith, these basic doctrines are almost all that is taught in the churches today. There are more than 20,000 sermons on baptism alone, on one sermon website alone, and new ones are coming out weekly. Whole conferences are put up every year on these same topics. In fact, this is how one attains to celebrity status in the modern evangelical world: repeat the same basic doctrines, the same milk of the faith, perhaps in fancier and fancier words,

---

33. R.J. Rushdoony, *Institutes of Biblical Law*, p. 766.
34. *Ibid.*

over and over again. Where new churches appear—often supposedly to right the wrongs of the established ones—the same things are preached again. In all respects, the American church today has not grown an inch in spiritual understanding beyond the original readers of Hebrews. Thus, it is an undisciplined church to start with. Such a church is in no position to practice "discipline" on anyone, and no formal "membership" in it can produce any kind of discipline.

Thus, true discipline is in true preaching and teaching the Word of God (John 15:3; 17:17; Eph. 5:26). But such preaching and teaching does not need formal church "membership," nor can it be restricted to the local congregation and its session. Nor can it be restricted to a handful of churchian bureaucrats and celebrities who have gathered a "congregation" around themselves. It comes from a wide variety of sources, including private study and even admonitions from prophets who may not be connected to any visible body. A truly disciplined church is focused on learning, not on institutional control.

Excommunication Is Not a Prerogative of Elders

This point may come as a deep surprise to many Christians today because of a mass of teachings we have simply inhereted and not questioned. Whatever teachings we may have inherited, it is our right *and duty* to judge by Scripture. When we go to Scripture, *we do not find a single verse that connects excommunication to elders.* In the places where the prerogatives of elders are listed, excommunication is not. In verses that deal with excommunication, elders are not mentioned. To start with, the main justification for excommunication in Matthew 18:15–20 does not mention elders or sessions or church leadership. The word used there is "the church." And in verse 20, Jesus declares His presence in His Church even where there are only two or three believers gathered together. We will see below what this means.

In Acts 6:4, the Apostles, acting as elders of the church in Jerusalem (which could not have been a "local church" given that it had thousands of believers at that time, and was meeting in each others' houses), described their duties as "prayer and the ministry of the Word." Excommunication is not mentioned. The focus is on teaching, in agreement with what was said above that true discipline is in learning, not punishments.

The sections in the Bible, however, which contain the lengthiest and most detailed exposition of the duties and prerogatives of elders are Paul's two epistles to Timothy and his epistle to Titus. It is common today, when qualifications and duties of eldership are mentioned, to focus only on a few verses in these epistles, where the minimum requirements are listed: 1 Tim. 3:1–7 and Titus 1:5–8. What is often missed is that Timothy and Titus were themselves elders, and these three epistles, in their entirety, are instructions to elders. In giving instructions to Timothy and Titus, Paul in fact gave instructions to all the elders and bishops of what their obligations and prerogatives are.

Surprisingly then, in all these thirteen chapters of detailed instructions to these two elders, Paul did not mention excommunication once. Keep in mind, Timothy and Titus were not simply elders, they were rather "super-elders" (bishops?), for they were charged with the task of *ordaining* elders. Not only were they "super-elders," they had a claim to true authority: both were appointed and ordained by Paul, and Timothy also had the authority of special prophecies behind him (1 Tim. 1:18; 4:14). If any elder ever in history could claim that his binding and loosing were God's binding and loosing, it would be these two men. Yet, in all his instructions, Paul mentioned nothing of excommunication.

These men were sent to their fields to bring discipline to the churches under their supervision (1 Tim. 1:3; Titus 1:5); that was the main purpose of their sending. Under the dominant ecclesiology in the modern churches, Paul would have given them a detailed list of judicial procedures for punishments and excommunication; just look at the book of discipline of any modern denomination, or listen to any sermon on church discipline. But there is nothing of the sort in Paul's epistles, not even a mention of it. What *is* mentioned over and over again is *instruction.*

In accordance with what we saw above, Paul saw instruction as the only instrument of discipline given to these "super-elders," Timothy and Titus. The verses are too many to quote, so I will just list them: 1 Timothy 1:5; 2:6; 3:2; 4:6, 11, 13, 16; 5:1, 7, 17; 6:2, 17; 2 Timothy 2:2, 14–15, 24–26; 4:1–2; Titus 1:9; 2:1, 15; 3:1, 14. Nothing is about excommunication; everything is about teaching; all is in the context of church discipline.

Thus, there is absolutely no Biblical foundation for the modern concept of excommunication as the prerogative of elders. Such concept is the fruit of extra-Biblical traditions, not of careful exegesis of the Bible. The duty of the elders is to teach, not to punish.

Excommunication Is a Prerogative of the Church

Because the modern view of discipline is so much focused on punishments, and so much revolves around "local church" hierarchy, one very clear Biblical truth is always missing from modern teachings on discipline: *excommunication is left in the hands of the Church in general, which means the individual believers, not their elders.* In every single place in the New Testament where excommunication is mentioned, the agency responsible for making the decision and enforcing it is not the church leadership but the mass of individual believers.

Starting with that most favorite passage of all advocates of excommunication with discipline, Matthew 18:15–20, here is what the verse has to say about the final stage:

> If he refuses to listen to them, tell it to the church; and if he refuses to listen even to the church . . . (v. 17).

But what is *the church* here? Is it the elite of church leaders? Not according to the Reformed confessions:

> The visible Church, which is also catholic or universal under the Gospel (not confined to one nation, as before under the law), consists of all those throughout the world that profess the true religion; and of their children. . . .[35]

It is tempting, of course, in the modern context, to assume that the "church" must be an official leadership body which issues verdicts and enforces them for the local church. But there is no support for such conclusion in the Bible. Besides Matthew 18, we have 1 Corinthians 5:9–13. In these verses, however, Paul speaks to the gathering of believers, not to their elders or their church session. We need to remember the words of Charles Hodge we quoted above:

> The Scriptures are everywhere addressed to the people, and not to the officers of the Church either exclusively, or specially. The prophets were sent to the people, and constantly said, "Hear, O Israel," "Hearken, O ye people." Thus, also, the discourses of Christ were addressed to the people, and the people heard him gladly. All the Epistles of the New Testament are addressed to the congregation, to the "called of Jesus Christ;" "to the beloved of God;" to those "called to be saints;" "to the sanctified in Christ Jesus;" "to all who call on the name of Jesus Christ our Lord;" "to the saints which are

35. WCF 25:2; cf. Belgic Confession 27; Second Helvetic Confession 17:1.

> in (Ephesus), and to the faithful in Jesus Christ;" or "to the saints and faithful brethren which are in (Colosse);" and so in every instance. It is the people who are addressed. To them are directed these profound discussions of Christian doctrine, and these comprehensive expositions of Christian duty. They are everywhere assumed to be competent to understand what is written, and are everywhere required to believe and obey what thus came from the inspired messengers of Christ.

Even more, the Corinthian church far from a very ordered and organized church. To the contrary, Paul's admonitions in chapters 12 and 14 show that there was a certain level of disorder he found necessary to correct. Yet, even in those chapters, Paul relies on his words and on the self-control of his readers; he mentions nothing of elders nor of church officers who should step in and institute order and discipline. The same applies to the excommunication case in chapter 5: Paul speaks to every one of those individual believers as the church. He expects everyone one of them to take his words and apply them. Paul does not issue the verdict, neither does he take upon himself the administration of that verdict. He only instructs. He expects his readers to judge and to decide for themselves who it is that claims to be a brother but is not.

Paul repeats the same admonition to another church in 2 Thessalonians 3:6:

> Now we command you, brethren, in the name of our Lord Jesus Christ, that you keep away from every brother who leads an unruly life and not according to the tradition which you received from us.

Again, elders are not mentioned anywhere in that epistle. The command is to the ordinary believers in the church.

They are supposed to exercise judgment, and they are supposed to execute that judgment. Excommunication by professional leaders is not mentioned.

We see an image of this communal excommunication in the requirement for communal execution for some crimes in the Law of God, for example, Leviticus 24:14 and Deuteronomy 21:21. The elders of the city or of the community were supposed to act as judges and declare the verdict, but there was no professional class of executors. It was left to the men of the community to stone the offender. This is presented today as some sort of primitive cruelty, but what most commentators fail to see that in this requirement of execution by the community rather by a government-hired hangman, there is a check and balance on judicial arbitrariness and injustice. If the judge was too harsh or corrupt, and if the community believed that the verdict was not just, the verdict may have remained on the books, but there would be no execution. Thus, there would be an ultimate check on the judge's actions, and that would be what would be called today "nullification by community restraint."

Similarly, in the New Testament church, the elders could be judges and could issue verdicts concerning the walk and the doctrines of some men. An example would be Paul in 1 Timothy 1:20, "delivering to Satan" certain men for their conduct and teachings. In the final account, however, the real action of excommunication was reserved not for the elders themselves—of which we have not a single biblical example, or even verse—but was left to the self-government and private judgment of the individual believers as the Church. Thus, excommunication was not a ceremonial nor an administrative action. It was a responsibility of the community, irrespective of the decisions of the elders.

Rushdoony wrote about this error in the modern church:

> *Fifth*, in terms of these ministerial powers, we have great authority, of binding and loosing. If two or

> three gathered together in Christ's name, either as a church court or as simple believers, agree on something in faithfulness to Scripture, we can bind and loose men. Now normally this is a function of church authorities.[36]

This concept of excommunication as a responsibility of the community also gives the solution to the question I asked above: "Who excommunicates the excommunicators?" Under the modern system, as we saw, a local church session cannot be excommunicated if it commits injustice. Under the Biblical concept of excommunication, a session can be excommunicated by the community over which it presides, despite any decisions of the session to the contrary, without the need of any other authority, by the private judgment and agreement of the ordinary members. This is actually happening today in the exodus of many Christians from visible institutional churches.[37] It is a mass excommunication of modern church leaders by Christians who want to remain faithful to the Word, are tired of being fed the same basic milk, and are exercising private judgment.

Thus, "local church membership" is not only not needed for excommunication, it is in fact harmful to the process of real Biblical excommunication because it binds the conscience of individual believers where God has not imposed any burdens, and insulates elders from accountability.

In addition, we may also point to the fact that where the Word is preached faithfully, the Bible expects the heretics, the teachers of false doctrines, to leave on their own accord, without the need for formal church discipline. In his first epistle, John speaks of the antichrists and their separation from the church:

---

36. R.J. Rushdoony, *Systematic Theology*, Vol. II, pp. 758–59.

37. See my article, "Kevin DeYoung's Gorbachevian Perestruvka Will Fail," http://bojidarmarinov.com/blog/kevin-deyoungs-gorbachevian-perestruvka-will-fail/

> Children, it is the last hour; and just as you heard that antichrist is coming, even now many antichrists have appeared; from this we know that it is the last hour. They went out from us, but they were not *really* of us; for if they had been of us, they would have remained with us; but *they went out,* so that it would be shown that they all are not of us. But you have an anointing from the Holy One, and you all know. I have not written to you because you do not know the truth, but because you do know it, and because no lie is of the truth (1 John 2:18–21).

Notice, *first,* that these false teachers were not kicked out, they *went out* on their own accord. *Second,* their going out is contrasted to the anointing and knowledge of those who remained in the church. As Rushdoony said concerning discipline in the church,

> There is a supernatural teaching or disciplining power inherent in the word of the supernatural God which is lacking in the words and actions of men.[38]

38. R.J. Rushdoony, *Institutes of Biblical Law,* p. 767.

13. Conclusion

I said at the beginning of this book that when Jeff Durbin made his statement against the "facebook prophets," he did not base it on the Bible or Reformed theology. Rather, he followed a relatively recent Baptist tradition which is popular today among the ministry-industrial complex. It is a tradition which seeks to chain individual Christians to obey and submit to men who often have no other credit except having received a degree or achieved certain levels of celebrity status. This is the same ministry-industrial complex which, for the last century, has made the church in America passive, powerless, and retreating on all fronts of the cultural war. When, however, we rise above the level of the propaganda and actually study the Bible, the historic church, and Reformed theology on the issue of "local church membership," we are forced to come to the following conclusions:

First, mandatory "local church membership" cannot be found as a principle in the Bible. A christian becomes a member of the Church in baptism. No other vow or covenant of membership is required of him. A member of the Church is equally a member of all local congregations. The Biblical principle is that an individual member's commitments follow his or her gifts and purpose before God, not any requirement to join a visible body—certainly not in the form of a mandatory local church "covenant." A member of a local body and a lone believer are equally legitimate members of the Church.

Sec*ond,* mandatory "local church membership" never existed as a concept in the church or in Reformed theology, and has only come to dominate the Reformed churches in the last one century. During prior centuries, it has always been characteristic to unorthodox cults, never to the Trinitarian churches.

Third, mandatory "local church membership" was introduced as a confessional standard among Reformed Baptists later in their history, and that as a concession to political pressure. It was not based on any specific Biblical example or command. Laying such an un-Biblical burden on the consciences of their followers, however, the authors of the Second London Baptist Confession created a contradiction that has caused problems for their churches ever since—were they to reason consistently.

Fourth, such fragmentation of the Church was the product of a pessimistic ideology which sees the Church as a permanent ghetto in a world which is a permanent den of evil. When the Church is optimistic about the Kingdom of God and its expansion into a Christian civilization, such focus on the local congregations is a waste of resources.

Fifth, contrary to the claims of the modern ministry-industrial complex, mandatory "local church membership" cannot be an effective tool for church discipline. To the contrary, it only encourages an undisciplined church because it elevates the power of the local sessions to the status of lack of accountability for the very leaders who are supposed to enforce the discipline. The history of the last one century—when the concept of mandatory "local church membership" became dominant—is an abundant evidence that the concept not only did not work, but also cannot work for the purposes it was supposedly introduced.

Sixth, the true Church is universal, and its bond of unity is the Word of God, not some visible institutional organization, global or local. It may include local congregations, but it also includes lone individuals who, for one reason or another, have chosen to remain separate from visible organizations. Membership in a visible body cannot be taken to be membership in the Church, and non-membership in a visible body does not automatically exclude a person from the Church. Making membership in a local visible body a standard for all believers is, according to Reformed theology, a Pelagian heresy and false worship. Any church teacher who teaches such a requirement is thereby guilty of false teaching, and as such should be ignored by his listeners. The standard for membership in a visible body or gathering with other Christians is left to Christian liberty; no burden can be laid on the conscience of the believer. Where there is some form of membership, the right and duty of private judgment trumps any obligation to a particular visible body. The local church is not "the Church," and it is not a even necessarily a "fundamental part" of the life of a Christian.

Seventh, church discipline is teaching and training, not punishments. Where there is no teaching or training, or where the people have been fed only the fundamental milk of the faith, there is no discipline. Excommunication is a very minuscule part of discipline, and it is not given as a prerogative to elders. It is a responsibility and a privilege of the whole church, of all the individuals in it; and subject to it must be first and foremost the very teachers and leaders in the church.

A specific application for the "facebook prophets" is this:

Your duty and obligation before God is to continue harassing the churchian leaders of our day, using all means available. Do not be intimidated by complaints or posts against you; the leaders most often do not know what they is talking about on this issue. Without you, all these ecclesiocrats would never experience any real church discipline; in the small churchdoms they have built for themselves, there is no way for them to be truly disciplined. You are their only check and balance. Only make sure your criticism and correction are in accordance with the Biblical message, your theology is sound and solid, and that you have your facts straight and are free of slander. As long as your opponents are complaining only about your "local church membership," you are safe, and they are in opposition to God, for He never asks His prophets who their elders are. So first make sure you are in agreement with the Word of God, and then . . . continue doing what you are doing.

The specific answer to all the leaders who would say otherwise can be found in the words of the great Dutch Reformed theologian, Herman Bavinck:

> It is not unbelievers primarily but the devout who have always experienced this power of the hierarchy as a galling bond to their consciences. Throughout the centuries there has not only been scientific, societal, and political resistance but also deeply religious and moral opposition to the hierarchical power of the church. It simply will not do to explain this opposition in terms of unbelief and disobedience and intentionally to misconstrue the religious motives underlying the opposition of various sects and movements. No one has been bold enough to damn all these sects because they were moved to resist the church and its tradition. Even Rome shrinks from this conclusion. The extra ecclesiam nulla salus (no salvation outside the church) is a confession that is too harsh for even the most robust believer. Accordingly, the "law" we see at work in every area of life is operative also in religion and morality. On the one hand, there is a revolutionary spirit that seeks to level all that has taken shape historically in order to start rebuilding things from the ground up. There is, however, also a false conservatism that takes pleasure in leaving the existing situation untouched simply because it exists and—in accordance with Calvin's familiar saying—not to attempt to change a well-positioned evil (malum bene positum non movere). At the proper time everywhere and in every sphere of life,

> a certain radicalism is needed to restore balance, to make further development possible, and not let the stream of ongoing life bog down. In art and science, state and society, similarly in religion and morality, there gradually develops a mindless routine that oppresses and does violence to the rights of personality, genius, invention, inspiration, freedom, and conscience. But in due time there always arises a man or woman who cannot bear that pressure, casts off the yoke of bondage and again takes up the cause of human freedom and that of Christian Liberty. These are turning points in history. Thus Christ himself rose up against the tradition of the elders and returned to the law and the prophets. Thus one day the Reformation had the courage, not in the interest of some scientific, social or political goal, but in the name of Christian humanity, to protest against Rome's hierarchy. . . .[39]

This quotation should be enough, but if anyone needs a Biblical warning, here it is:

> So in the present case, I say to you, stay away from these men and let them alone, for if this plan or action is of men, it will be overthrown; but if it is of God, you will not be able to overthrow them; or else you may even be found fighting against God (Acts 5:38–39).

In general, ministers, keep this in mind: every time you defend an institutional system against prophets, you are at risk before God. Especially if it is like the current one you are defending. It would be much safer before God to listen to the prophets, even if they are only on Facebook.

---

39. Herman Bavinck, *Reformed Dogmatics*, Vol. I, pp. 80–82.

CPSIA information can be obtained
at www.ICGtesting.com
Printed in the USA
FSOW03n0428080217
30479FS

9 781635 870398